PERSIAN MYTHOLOGY

PERSIAN MYTHOLOGY

JOHN R HINNELLS

HAMLYN

COLOUR PLATES

To my parents.
'I can no other answer make but thanks,
And thanks, and ever thanks.'
Shakespeare

The Hamlyn Publishing Group Limited
London New York Sydney Toronto
Hamlyn House, Feltham, Middlesex, England

ISBN 0 600 03090 3

Filmset by Filmtype Services Limited,
Scarborough, England
Manufactured in the United States of America

CONTENTS

The Zagros mountains, which form a mighty barrier to the west of Persia. This photograph illustrates more vividly than any words the difficulties faced by invading armies from the west.

Author's Note

The country traditionally referred to as 'Persia' is more correctly titled 'Iran'. The popular name of the country has been retained in this book in the belief that it will be more meaningful to most people. As Iran designates the land of the Aryans and has been the official title of the country for over twenty years 'Iranian mythology' would be the more correct title, albeit less widely understood.

Publisher's Note

The sources of quotations are given in abbreviated form throughout the book. For further information the reader is referred to the List of Abbreviations and the Bibliography.

INTRODUCTION

Persia is a land of great contrasts: a land of deserts and jungle, of snowy mountains and luxuriant valleys; a place where apples and date palms grow within miles of each other; a land of oil wells and nomads.

Three mountain ranges form a triangle around the land–mountains which rise to a height of 18,000 feet. At the heart of Persia lie two vast salt deserts. Within the mountain ranges are valleys, some as much as sixty miles long and twelve miles wide, with a climate like that of the Mediterranean countries. To the north, bordering the Caspian sea, lies dense tropical jungle. Rainfall varies from sixty inches a year in some parts to none in others. Although Persia has vast natural resources, it is only in recent times that they have been exploited, and apart from the famed 'Persian market place', agriculture is the traditional occupation.

Geography inevitably affects culture, and it is not surprising that in Persia there are a number of different cultures–cultures which in their turn have produced different mythologies. People in western Persia have always been open to influence from such centres as Greece and Rome, whereas those in the east have been influenced more by India and the Orient. Persia forms both a historical and a geographical bridge between East and West.

Our subject is that rich mine of poetry, folklore and myth which constituted much of the faith of ancient Persia. After a brief look at the history of Persia, the nature of our sources and the character of myth, we shall turn first to the ancient picture of the universe, the 'pagan' myths and the stories of the godly heroes fighting horrific dragons. Then we shall look at the highly ethical teaching of Zoroastrianism with its profound interpretation of traditional mythology. Once the national faith of Persia, Zoroastrianism is still devoutly practised by small communities in Persia, and also by the Parsis in India.

Persia has been the home of a number of religious traditions, we shall examine the mythology of two of them, Zurvanism and Mithraism. Finally we shall consider the part mythology has played in the ritual, history and court of the land of the shahs. Most important of all, we shall try to understand the place of myth in the personal faith of the believer. This book, then, is concerned with both ancient and modern times, with history and with a living faith, albeit a small and sadly decreasing one. Space will not, unfortunately, permit us to examine all the different faiths which have moved into Persia, such as the Mandeans, Manicheans or Muslims.

Outline of Persian History

No nation's religion or mythology can be understood in isolation from its historical setting; some knowledge is needed of the cultural developments and the various influences that were at work. Thus we must turn first to the history of Persia.

In the distant past the peoples now inhabiting Europe, Persia and India were all part of one group of tribes now referred to as the Indo-Europeans. Living perhaps in Central Europe, they gradually splintered off to form nations of their own. The Aryans, part of this complex of peoples, travelled south east, and in the second and first millenniums BC invaded India and Persia. We must not imagine one vast organised army, but rather small tribal groups settling down independently until, after centuries, they became so numerous that they dominated the land.

The peoples who settled in India and Persia are known as the Indo-Iranians. Their religion is preserved in the collection of ancient Hindu hymns, the *Rig Veda,* and the ancient Persian hymns, the *Yashts*. Their religion reflected their way of life as nomads and warriors. They delighted in the beauty of nature, yet stood in fear of its venom and apparent malice; hymns dwell on the beauty of the dawn, and the terror of the drought. Their gods are either personifications of such ideals as Truth, or of natural phenomena such as the storm, or they are swash-buckling heroes who destroy the monsters which threaten men, Indra and Keresaspa for example (see pp. 34, 43, 46). Although

The peacock theme in Persian art stems from India. This plate, together with those on pages 22, 28 and 35 illustrating adaptations of Chinese, Assyrian and Hellenistic styles, show the variety of influences to which Persia was subject.

both India and Persia have adapted and developed their beliefs far beyond this heritage, it is remarkable how much it still dominates their myth and ritual. Because the settlement of the Indo-Iranians was such a gradual affair, and archaeological remains are naturally so few, it is difficult to date with any precision their conquest of the land; however, by 800 BC they appear to have been dominant.

Zoroaster, (the name is the Greek form of the Persian Zarathushtra) was the great prophet of Persia. He is traditionally dated c. 628–551 BC, although he may have lived centuries before this. It is generally thought that his home was in the Central Asian steppes. His teachings have been handed down over the centuries in his hymns, the *Gathas*. Zoroaster was himself a priest and the *Gathas* are composed in a traditional style and metre which resembles that of the ancient Indian *Vedas*. His thought, however, is considerably different. He obviously knew the traditional mythology, but what strikes the reader of the *Gathas* is the abstract manner in which he interprets it. He speaks, for example, of seven beings, the Bounteous Immortals, who are sons and daughters of God, Ahura Mazda, but their character is shown by their names, the Holy (or Bounteous) Spirit, Good Mind, Truth, Kingdom, Devotion, Integrity and Immortality. They are all aspects of God in which man can share if he follows the path of Truth (or the word used, *Asha,* could be translated Righteousness), for the path of Truth will lead men to Good Mind and Devotion, through which they achieve Integrity, Immortality and the Kingdom. Only the Holy or Creative Spirit belongs exclusively to God. Zoroaster also speaks of saviours, but he does not appear to think of them so much as mythological beings, rather as those who through justice and truth overcome passion and spread the Good Religion, so establishing the

The winged symbol of Ahura Mazda on a relief at Persepolis.

A lion's head from the top of a column at Persepolis. The lion is a traditional symbol of power.

A griffin's head from one of the columns at Persepolis.

Kingdom of God on earth. This should not lead one to categorise Zoroaster as a philosopher rather than a religious prophet; few men have been more aware of the presence of God. In the *Gathas* Zoroaster addresses Ahura Mazda as 'friend', for he is convinced that God will give him 'friendly support'. Ahura Mazda is the one who set Zoroaster apart from the beginning for his mission. He was conscious above all of the goodness of God and attributed all physical and moral evil to the devil, Angra Mainyu, the Spirit of Destruction, the Evil Mind.

Because the prophet's own teaching appears to have been so abstract it would be misleading to include a chapter on it in a book on mythology. What we will do instead is to look at the way in which the figure of Zoroaster has been treated in later tradition.

The teaching of Zoroaster at first aroused great opposition, but when he succeeded in converting a local chieftain, Vishtaspa, Zoroastrianism began to spread. When it became the religion of the court of the King of Kings we do not know. The great Persian empire of the Achaemenids was founded by Cyrus the Great, who began as ruler of a small kingdom, Anshan, in south-west Persia. After invading Egypt and Lydia in Asia Minor and marching east into India, he turned his attention to the mighty empire of Babylon which, divided and demoralised, opened up its gates to the conqueror without offering any resistance. United for the first time, Persia was transformed by one man into one of the greatest empires the world has ever known. The policy of Cyrus and his successors towards the subject peoples was one of tolerance. They were given a remarkable degree of autonomy and were allowed to follow their own religions.

Although Cyrus was the founder of the Achaemenid empire, its great

*A bull's head which decorated the top of a column in the great hall at Persepolis (*in situ*). The bull is a widespread symbol of vitality and fertility.*

right *A relief from the treasury at Persepolis. The great king Darius is shown lifted up on his throne, holding the insignia of office, the lotus and sceptre. Before the king stand two fire altars or incense burners. The figure behind the throne is the crown prince, Xerxes. His royal dignity is shown by the lotus he carries, and his association with the crown by his act of touching the royal throne.*

below right *These winged creatures, which stand at the gatehouse of Xerxes I, symbolise the might of the invincible king of kings. The Assyrian influence on these enormous figures is clear.*

below *A four-winged genius on a jamb of the gateway at Pasargadae. Above the figure there was an inscription, now destroyed, which declared in three languages: 'I, Cyrus, the king, the Achaemenid [built this].' The genius, carved in the simple manner which was typical of the early period, was thought to be a protective spirit guarding the entrance to the royal residence.*

designer was Darius (521–486 BC). It may be that he was a usurper, we cannot be sure, but he was certainly a great military leader and administrator. A fervent disciple of truth and justice, he drew up a law code for the empire. As well as leaving for history the great palace at Persepolis, Darius has also left us many inscriptions which expound his understanding of his position as king. He refers constantly to the fact that it is by the grace of Ahura Mazda that he is king, and that it is he who gives success to Darius. All who oppose the king are of the 'Lie'. These inscriptions have been taken by many to show that by the time of Darius Zoroaster's teaching had permeated the empire and converted the King of Kings himself. Although the inscriptions make no reference to some of the central Zoroastrian teachings, the Bounteous Immortals for example, they do suggest a religious belief similar to that of the great prophet.

It was under Darius and his successor, Xerxes, that the famed invasions of Greece were attempted and the first 'marathon' was run. Towards the end of Xerxes' reign (d. 465 BC) Persian military power began to decline, but it was not for another hundred years, until the rise of the mighty Alexander the Great, that she fell. The empire of the King of Kings was apparently drowned in the tide of Hellenism, yet Persia had no small influence on her conquerors.

In the third century BC the fight for independence began, and by 150 BC the Parthian empire emerged under Mithradates. The Parthians came from north-eastern Iran, not from Persia proper. In the early stages of their rule they made great use of Hellenic technical resources in their architecture, coinage and art, but as they gained experience and skill their national heritage emerged more and more clearly.

The Sasanians, with their base in Persia proper, overthrew the Parthians in

The tomb of Cyrus on the southern edge of the site at Pasargadae. Made of blocks of fine white limestone, it has the appearance of marble. The funerary chamber is thirty-six feet high and the lowest 'step' is the height of a man. The tomb is still revered by Persian Muslims as 'the tomb of Solomon's mother'.

Maitreya Buddha, the Buddha to come at the close of the age. Some scholars believe that this concept was influenced by the Zoroastrian belief in the saviour, Soshyant.

AD 224. Under Shapur I (ruled c. 240–272) Persian armies invaded east through the Hindu Kush into India and the Kushan kingdom and westwards to Antioch in Syria and Cappadocia. There was an enormous problem in uniting such an empire, containing as it did so many different religious groups in the homeland itself: Zoroastrians, Zurvanites, Manicheans, Hindus, Buddhists, Greeks, Jews, Christians and pagans. The Christians in particular were a politically suspect group after the conversion of the ruler of Persia's greatest enemy, Constantine, to Christianity. Manicheism, a syncretistic cult, seemed to offer a possible solution to the problem, but largely as a result of the efforts of Kartir, a particularly vigorous defender of the Zoroastrian faith and a great power behind the throne, Zoroastrianism was confirmed as the state religion.

The political and economic history of Sasanian Persia resembles a swinging pendulum. In the fifth century Persia was torn internally by the rise of Mazdakism, an abortive form of communism, and in 484 the country was invaded from the east by the Ephthalites. In 531, Khusrau I, perhaps the country's greatest ruler, came to the throne. He defeated the Ephthalites and invaded Syria, but his greatest achievements were in the field of internal reform. He re-established the power of the monarchy, introduced fiscal, agricultural, social and military reform, the state control of education and a vast building programme. The stability which he achieved within the society was so great that it led eventually to the stagnation and decay of the state. The king himself was so revered by his people that the legend grew up that he had passed deathless into the hereafter and that he would return at the end of the world with an army to defeat the demons who would attack Persia.

In 610 Sasanian Persia gave to the world her swansong. Her armies swept westwards to the Bosphorus, Constantinople, Damascus, Jerusalem, Gaza and Egypt, all within the space of six years (610–616). But despite this outstanding military success, which gave Persia the appearance of a world-conquering power for centuries to come, she fell before the Islamic invasion in 651. Torn by internal strife, corrupt and stagnant, Persia could not withstand the passionate assault of the warrior missionaries of the world's latest faith.

After the initial bloodbath there was less systematic persecution of Zoroastrianism than many books imply. There was, however, a flood of converts to

This series of coins illustrates something of the development in coinage from Achaemenid to Sasanian times. The first coin, a fifth-century Achaemenid gold daric, shows a warrior not unlike the archers at Susa. The second, an early Parthian silver drachma, is thought to show the head of king Mithradates I (c. 171–138 BC). He is clean-shaven, following Hellenic fashion. The third coin is from the reign of Mithradates II (128–88 BC), showing the king bearded in Persian fashion. The reverse of the coin shows Arsaces, the deified ancestor of the Parthians. On the last two coins (a drachma of Shapur I, AD 241–272, and a gold denarius of Khusrau II, AD 590–628) the kings are shown wearing the ornate crowns of the Sasanian period. The modelling of the hair is similar in style to that on some of the Sasanian reliefs. Khusrau wears a crown with wings resembling the symbol for the god Verethraghna and the symbol of the moon god, Mah. He is also set against the background of the sun and moon, for the king is a cosmic figure. It is, then, not only the style but also the thought that has developed from the simplicity of the Achaemenid coin.

Islam. Perhaps it was the vitality of Islam compared with what has been described as 'the decaying ritualism of a state church' (Frye), and not simply persecution which attracted Persians to the new faith; we cannot say. Persia to this day remains a devoutly Muslim country with about 17,000 Zoroastrians, mainly in Tehran, Yazd and Kerman. Many of the faithful emigrated to India where they form the community of the Parsis (Persians). Now centred mainly on Bombay, the Parsis number some 120,000. Since converts are not accepted the number of believers in the faith first taught some 2,500 years ago in the Central Asian steppes is dwindling steadily.

The Sources of the Myths

Our knowledge of the mythology of Persia is derived from a variety of sources. The most important of these is the Zoroastrian bible, the *Avesta*. Unfortunately only that part of the *Avesta* which is used in the ritual has survived, approximately one quarter of the original. Although it was not written down in its final form until Sasanian times the contents are considerably older. Indeed, within the general Zoroastrian structure of the *Avesta* are reflected and preserved ancient, pre-Zoroastrian myths.

The most important part of this complex of material is the *Gathas,* the seventeen hymns of Zoroaster. Although they are exceedingly difficult to translate the profundity of their teaching makes them rank among the most precious gems of the world's religious literature.

The *Gathas* are embedded in the *Yasna,* a collection of prayers and invocations chanted during the Zoroastrian sacrifice of the same name. These texts are of diverse origins and date: one section, for example, is a pre-Zoroastrian hymn to the god Haoma (*Ys. 9–11,* see below p. 38), whereas others are evidently Zoroastrian compositions.

For the purpose of this book one of the most important sections of the *Avesta* is that which embodies the twenty-four *Yashts* or hymns to various gods. Although all these hymns are used in the Zoroastrian services many of them basically date back to the pre-Zoroastrian period. One such hymn is *Yasht 10,* the hymn to Mithra, which we shall look at later.

Other sections of the *Avesta* are concerned with ritual directions, more prayers and invocations. This whole collection of ritual material is preserved in a dead church language, Avestan, which few priests understand, but because the words are thought to have effective power it is important to them that every 'jot and tittle' is preserved. It is this reverence for the sacred word which has enabled the material to be preserved for so long without suffering much corruption.

The Pahlavi, or Middle Persian literature, embodies a great variety of types of material: expositions and defence of the faith, visionary and apocalyptic material, wisdom and epic literature, poetry and historical works. Many of them naturally reflect the thought of the age in which they were written, but some preserve the myths and beliefs of the *Avesta*. One text for example, the *Bundahishn,* is a collection of translations of Avestan texts on the act, nature and goal of creation. The work includes, of course, later scribal comment, and in using this book it will be important to try to syphon such material away, but long passages appear to reflect accurately the thought of ancient Persia. Large sections of another work, the *Denkard,* simply summarise the contents of the *Avesta*. Within this one block of material, then, we have not only the theology, hopes and fears of the Zoroastrians faced with Muslim rule, but also the myths of pre-Zoroastrian Persia.

A number of Islamic historians showed an interest in the ancient history and beliefs of the conquered peoples, and we have a number of Islamic presentations of Persian mythology. The main one we shall refer to in this book is the *Shah name,* an enormous work written by the poet, Firdausi. Firdausi turned a prose reconstruction of Persian history from the day of creation to the Islamic conquest into verse form. His source, now unfortunately lost, interpreted myths as historical narratives, so that many of the mythical gods or heroes appear as 'historical' kings or heroes. Although he suppresses most of

A silver drachma showing Ardashir I, the founder of the Sasanian empire. The fire altar on the reverse is interesting for its claw-shaped feet.

those elements of the tradition which would be offensive to his Islamic readers, the author reproduces beautifully the spirit of the Zoroastrian texts. Much of the narrative retains a sense of the underlying significance of the cosmic battle between forces of good and evil, presenting it as an earthly battle between good kings and tyrants.

Turning further afield, we shall have to use the sacred texts of ancient India, the *Vedas,* particularly the collection of hymns known as the *Rig Veda.* These hymns were written down at a very late date but their content goes back to the period 1500–500 BC. Although some allowance must be made for the influence of the indigenous beliefs, the *Vedas* appear to preserve many of the beliefs of the ancient Indo-Iranians and so they can be used, albeit cautiously, in reconstructing the faith of pre-Zoroastrian Persia.

These are the main sources we shall use, but there are many more: the inscriptions of the Persian Kings, the reports of classical and foreign authors, art, coins, reliefs and of course archaeology. But we must not expect too much from our various sources. Ritual texts, particularly hymns, whichever religion they belong to, rarely try to give a thorough explanation of a belief; they hint at or allude to teachings or myths the worshipper knows well. They move his heart rather than exercise his brain. The hymns we are using naturally make many allusions which we miss completely. Nor must we expect too much from the reports of classical and foreign authors: how accurate would a picture of Christianity be that was built up from the comments of outside observers? Evidence from art and coins is often ambiguous; if the same pictorial symbol can mean different things to different believers, how much more so to scholars from a different culture centuries after they were executed! The reconstruction of myth is often, therefore, a matter of debate among scholars. In this book controversial points have been avoided or noted wherever possible, reserving further discussion of such problems for purely academic studies.

above *Buddhist fresco from the caves at Bamiyan, Afghanistan. From the first to the seventh centuries AD Bamiyan was a Buddhist stronghold, although there was a great deal of Persian influence on the iconography.*

right *The Chinese influence on this scene from the* Shah name, *showing the famous king Bahram Gur fighting the dragon, is clear.*

far right *An illustration from a manuscript of the Hindu epic text, the* Mahabharata, *showing the figure of Kalki, the incarnation of the god Vishnu which is expected at the end of history. A number of scholars believe that the figure of Kalki was influenced by the Zoroastrian belief in a saviour to come.*

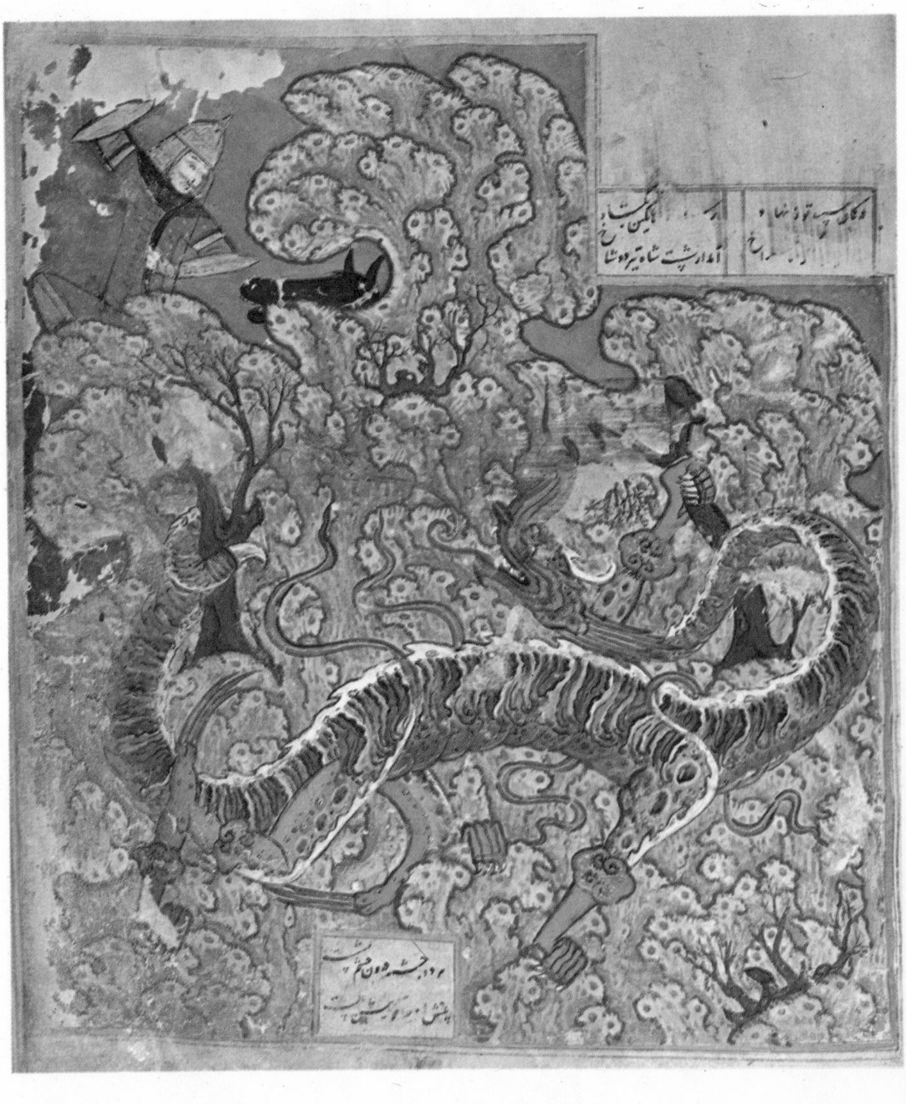

A large statue of the Buddha, fifty-three metres high, from Bamiyan, Afghanistan. This monumental rock carving, dating from the fourth or fifth century AD, serves as an example of the different religious traditions which were to be found in lands bordering on Persia. The immensity of the carving expresses the belief that Buddha is the lord of the world.

The Nature of Myth

Before we turn to the mythology of Persia we shall do well to pause and consider the actual nature of myth. In everyday language 'myth' has come to mean that which is fanciful or untrue, a usage encouraged by the Oxford English Dictionary which begins its definition with the words 'Purely fictitious narrative . . .' This approach is completely misleading. It assumes that myths should be viewed as quasi-factual stories which are either true or false. But precisely what is meant by 'true'? In Aesop's fable of the fox and the grapes it does not matter whether the narrative is factually accurate, it is the significance and meaning of the moral that is important. In some ways myths are rather similar. What is important is not the historical accuracy of the narratives, but what they mean to the believer. It is their function in religion which distinguishes myths from fables. In his religion man attempts to explain his understanding of himself, of his nature and his environment. Myths, containing, in narrative form, man's reflections on existence, are the standard forms in which he expresses this understanding. A creation myth is more important for its reflections on the nature of the world, man or God, than as a rival to Darwin's theories concerning evolution. A myth of the virgin birth of a prophet or saviour is not important as a historical account of the mother's love-life, but rather as an expression of the place of the prophet or saviour in the faith of the believer.

Not only are myths expressions of man's reflections on the basic meaning of life, they are also charters by which he lives, and they can act as the *rationale* of a society. The established pattern of society is given its ultimate authority through mythical concepts, whether they be the concepts of the divine right of kings in Stuart England, or the tri-partite pattern of society in Indo-Iranian belief. This taught that the gods created society with a three-fold structure: some men were created priests, others warriors and a third group were created productive workers, so that all men owed their station in life to the will of the gods. Myths can function equally as exhortations to a high moral code and provide men with models by which they fashion their own lives.

But myths are much more than mere narratives or symbolic accounts. Because they relate the activity of the supernatural they are held to release or re-activate that power as they are recited in the ritual. As Christians believe that by ritually re-enacting the Last Supper in the Communion service Christ is made present for the believer, so people of other religions believe that by dramatising a myth of creation, of (as in Persia) the final sacrifice to be offered by the saviour, that same power active at creation or at the end is made present for the faithful. Through myth and ritual the presence of the sacred is secured.

Myths, then, provide charters for ethical and religious conduct, they express and codify beliefs, they are sources of supernatural power. Thus in looking at Persian mythology we are not looking simply at bogus historical narratives, nor just at beautiful and ancient poetry (though myth is often that as well). We are looking at the basic Persian world view, its understanding of man, society and God.

If a myth is to be effective as a symbol then it must employ terms and imagery meaningful to its hearers. The other side of the coin is, of course, that the imagery will not be meaningful to those of another culture. The danger, therefore, in re-telling myths in their original form is that a foreigner may seize on those elements which appear bizarre and so miss the deeper insights which lie behind the symbols. The readers may, in other words, look at the symbol and not at what is symbolised. The last part of this book will, therefore, leave the outer shell of myth behind and look at the kernel, the understanding of man and the world in Persian mythology.

A roundel found near Ziwiye showing the divine Gilgamesh lifting lions, a motif which is found in later Achaemenid seals applied to the kings. It may be only the iconography which the Persians took over, but it is interesting that motifs belonging to gods could be applied to kings. It is possible that belief in the divinity of the king existed in Achaemenid as well as in Sasanian Persia.

A detail of the ninth–eighth century bowl from Hasanlu (see page 30) showing the charioteer gods.

ANCIENT PERSIAN MYTHOLOGY

The Picture of the Universe

The ancient Persians thought of the world as round and flat, like a plate. The sky, to them, was not infinite space, but a hard substance, like rock crystal, which encompassed the world like a shell. In its original perfect state the earth was flat, with no valleys or mountains, and the sun, moon and constellations stood still over the earth at the noonday position. All was peaceful and harmonious. But this tranquil state was shattered by the entry of evil into the universe. It crashed in through the sky, plunged down into the waters and then burst up through the centre of the earth, causing the earth to shake and the mountains to grow. The chief mountain was Mount Alburz which took eight hundred years to grow. For two hundred years it grew to the star station; for two hundred it grew to the moon station; for two hundred it grew to the sun station, and for the final two hundred it grew to the utmost limit of the sky. The mountain thus spreads through the cosmos, while its base is attached to the sky where it encloses the world. The roots of this cosmic mountain spread under the earth, holding it together, and from these roots grow all the other mountains. In the middle of the earth stands Mount Tera, the peak of Alburz, and from there to heaven stretches the Chinvat bridge over which all souls must pass at death on their journey to heaven or hell. The Arezur ridge on the rim of Mount Alburz is the gateway to hell where the demons discourse.

It was not only the earth that was shaken by the entry of evil into the universe. The sun, moon and constellations were shaken from their place so that they revolve round the earth like crowns until the renovation of the universe, entering the sky each day through one of the hundred and eighty apertures on Mount Alburz in the east, and setting through one of the hundred and eighty apertures in the west.

The rains were formed by the god Tishtrya (see pp. 31–2). They were blown together by the wind to form the cosmic ocean, Vourukasha, or boundless ocean, which lies beyond the peak of Mount Alburz. This ocean is so wide that it contains a thousand lakes, the springs of the goddess Anahita (see pp. 32–3). Within the ocean stand two trees, the tree of many seeds, from which all other trees derive, and the Gaokerena tree, or White Hom, from which all men will receive the elixir of immortality at the renovation of the universe. Evil

In 1947 a shepherd boy in Kurdistan discovered a priceless hoard of treasure on a mountainside. This treasure of Ziwiye had been buried beneath the walls of a citadel sometime in the seventh century BC *when enemies, probably the Scythians, had attacked the palace.*

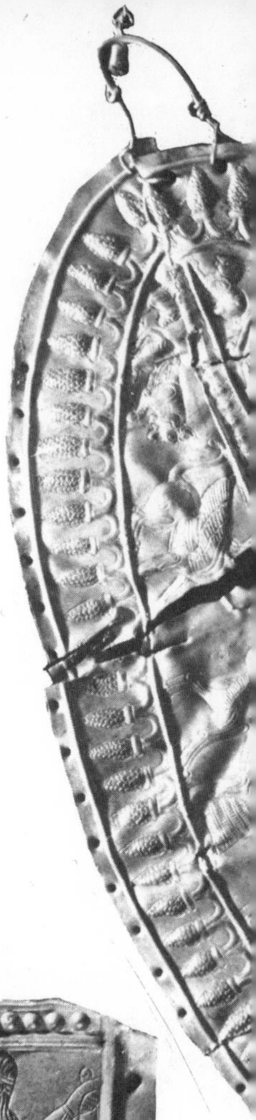

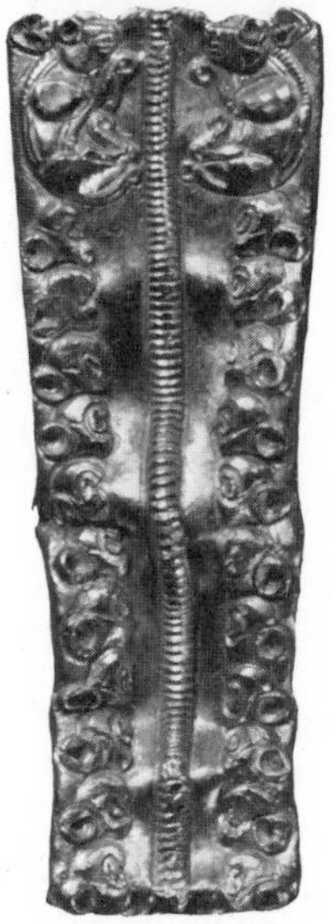

above *These three pieces are from gold plaques and a dagger belt cover; the belts have been thought to have some magical significance. The repoussé work on the largest fragment involved a new technique in goldwork. The style shows both Scythian and Anatolian influence.*

right *The theme of a warrior and lion fighting, seen on the embossed and engraved gold plaque, is typically Assyrian. The motif and style are found again in later Iranian art. Although this plaque is very decorative the original intention was probably more than mere decoration; the scene may depict a ritual combat.*

top right *The scenes on the crescent-shaped pectoral are divided into two registers. The mythological monsters are largely derived from Assyrian imagery, for example, the winged bull with a human head. Perhaps the most interesting feature is the symbolic world tree at the centre. A mythological tree appears in many religions, including that of the Persians. As in much ancient Near-Eastern symbolism the demons' bodies are composed of parts from different animals.*

bottom right *Battles between dignitaries in chariots and roaring lions is a common theme in the art of the period. The scene on the right-hand side of the ivory plaque continues and is linked to a scene showing an ibex and a sacred tree.*

naturally tried to destroy this life-giving tree and formed a lizard to attack it, but it is protected by ten *kar*, fish which swim ceaselessly round in such a way that one of them is always watching the lizard.

Then three great and twenty small seas were formed. Two rivers ran through the earth, one running from the north to the west and the other from the north to the east, both eventually running over the ends of the earth, mingling again with the cosmic ocean.

When the rains first came the earth split into seven pieces. The central portion, Khwanirath, forms one half of the total land mass and the surrounding six portions are referred to as the Keshvars. Men were unable to pass from one region to another unless they rode on the back of the heavenly bull, Srishok, or Hadhayos. Srishok is carefully watched over by the righteous Gopatshah, half man and half ox, for he is to be the last animal to be offered in sacrifice at the renovation when all men are to be made immortal.

The bull is not the only remarkable creature in this ancient picture of the universe. An even more fantastic animal is the three-legged ass. Where it came from we do not know, nor do we know what the mythical beast was meant to be. One scholar has suggested that it was originally part of a meteorological myth since it is said to shake the waters of the cosmic ocean; others believe that it was originally a foreign god incorporated into Persian belief. Whatever its origin, this holy animal is said to have three feet, six eyes, nine mouths, two ears and a horn. It is as big as a mountain and each foot covers as much ground as a thousand sheep; its task is to destroy the worst disease and pests.

The Ancient Gods

Worship was offered not in a cathedral or temple but in the open air on the mountain tops. The ancient Persians used

A bowl from Hasanlu, dated ninth–eighth century BC. The top frieze shows a procession of weather gods in chariots. Underneath are a series of scenes from a cycle of Hurrian myths. In the centre can be seen a hero fighting a god of the mountains.

to ascend to the highest peaks of the mountains, and offer sacrifices to Zeus, calling the whole vault of the sky, Zeus; and they sacrifice also to Sun, Moon, Earth, Fire, Water and Winds.
Herodotus, 1,131, M.EZ pp. 391f.

Their altars are not to be found in temples, but high up in the mountains, and the great reliefs and inscriptions of the kings are found not in large centres of civilisations but on the rock faces of mountains.

Although the gods are often described in mythical imagery, there are remarkably few myths related about them. They may be described in anthropomorphic terms, as charioteer gods who drive forth in beautiful golden chariots pulled by immortal horses, but as soon as one looks at the anthropomorphism closely it dissolves. The great god Mithra, for example, is said to have one thousand eyes, a piece of vivid symbolism which expresses the conviction that no man can conceal his wrongdoing from the god and evade the consequences.

Many scholars believe that as Indo-European society was divided into three classes–rulers, warriors and productive workers–so too were the gods. This theory of the 'tri-partite' structure of human and divine society has been used as a key to unlock many of the problems of ancient Persian mythology, probably too many, but it is quite credible that the divine hierarchy was fashioned on the basis of the human model.

There were a great many gods in the mythology of the ancient Persians, more than can be discussed here. All we can do is to look at the main figures in Indo-Iranian and native Persian thought.

Vayu, Wind

The wind, bringer of life in the rain cloud and of death in the storm, is one of the most mysterious gods of the Indo-Iranians. In an Indian text he is said to come from the breath of the world giant out of whose body the world was made. He rides in a swift-running chariot drawn by a hundred or even a thousand horses. It is he who produces 'the ruddy lights'–the lightning–and makes the dawn appear.

In Persia he is a great yet enigmatic figure. Both the creator (Ahura Mazda) and the devil (Angra Mainyu) offer sacrifice to him. The creator offered up a sacrifice on a golden throne under golden beams covered by a golden canopy, asking that he might smite the evil creation and that the good creation might be preserved. The prayers of the creator were granted, but the destructive desires of the devil were frustrated. Men also pray to Vayu, especially in times of peril, for he is a fearsome broad-breasted warrior. Wearing 'the raiment of warfare' and carrying a sharp spear and weapons made of gold, he ventures forth to pursue his enemies, to destroy the Evil Spirit and protect the good creation of Ahura Mazda.

Whereas Ahura Mazda rules above in light and Angra Mainyu below in darkness, Vayu rules in the intermediate space, the Void. There is a sense of the 'neutrality' of Vayu, for there is both a good and an evil Vayu. Some scholars believe that in later thought he was divided into two figures, but in the early period there is the idea of one figure embodying the dual features of a beneficent yet sinister, awesome power, the pitiless one who is associated with death, whose paths no one can escape. If he is properly propitiated he will deliver men from all assaults, for the wind moves through both worlds, the world of the Good Spirit and the world of the Evil Spirit. He is the worker of good, the destroyer, the one who unites, the one who separates. His name is 'he that goes forwards, he that goes backwards, he that hurls away, he that hurls down'. He is the most valiant, the strongest, the firmest and the stoutest.

Tishtrya and the Demon of Drought

Tishtrya is another figure associated with a natural phenomenon, the rains, but there is no sense of a duality in this god's character. He is a beneficent force involved in a cosmic battle against the life-destroying demon of drought, Apaosha. Tishtrya is 'the bright and glorious star', the first star, the seed of the waters, the source of rain and fertility.

Oado, the Kushana wind god, probably derived from the Persian Vata, the active element over which Vayu presides. The Kushan empire extended from the Ganges into Central Asia during the first three centuries AD. Their religion was subject to Chinese, Indian, Persian and Roman influences; thus many of the deities represented on their coins are taken from Persian religion.

Kanishka, the third Kushana king to issue coins. The dates of this famed king are a matter of debate; early second century AD is perhaps the most favoured. A great patron of Buddhism, Kanishka is the subject of a number of legends.

This coin of Kanishka's bears the first definite image of Buddha (here Boddo) to appear on a coin.

Sarapo, the Kushana representation of Serapis seated on a throne.

The fourth month of the year, June-July time, is dedicated to Tishtrya. In the first ten days of the month he is said to take the form of a man of fifteen–the ideal age in Persian thought. In the second ten days he takes the form of a bull and in the third ten days the form of a horse. According to the *Bundahishn* it was Tishtrya in these forms who produced the water at the beginning of creation. Each drop of rain he produced became as big as a bowl so that the earth was covered with water to the height of a man. The noxious creatures were forced to go into the holes of the earth, and the wind spirit then swept the waters to the borders of the earth, thus forming the cosmic ocean.

In a hymn dedicated to Tishtrya the battle between the god and the demon of drought is retold. Tishtrya went down to the cosmic ocean in the shape of a beautiful white horse with golden ears and golden trappings. There he met the demon Apaosha in the shape of a black horse, terrifying in appearance with his black ears and tail. Hoof against hoof they fought for three days and nights, but it was Apaosha who proved the stronger, and Tishtrya 'in woe and distress' cried out to the creator, Ahura Mazda, that he was weak because men had not been offering him the proper prayers and sacrifices. The creator himself then offered a sacrifice to Tishtrya, who was infused with the strength of ten horses, ten camels, ten bulls, ten mountains and ten rivers. Again Tishtrya and Apaosha met hoof against hoof but this time, fortified by the power of the sacrifice, Tishtrya proved triumphant and the waters were able to flow down unrestrained to the fields and pastures. Rain clouds rising from the cosmic ocean were propelled by the wind, and the life-giving rains poured down on the seven regions of the earth.

The *Bundahishn* and the hymn to Tishtrya present Tishtrya's lifegiving act in different lights. In the *Bundahishn* Tishtrya is the primeval producer of rain, seas and lakes. In the *Yasht* the emphasis is more on Tishtrya as the continual source of water in the annual cycle of nature, the giver of offspring, the one who defeats sorcerers, the lord of all stars and the protector of the Aryan lands. The importance of the being or star who presides over the time when the rains fall can only be appreciated if one remembers the great scourge of summer heat and drought which threatens a country with vast expanses of desert.

The myth of the battle with Apaosha also tells us something of the way in which the ancient Persians viewed the ritual. They believed that the gods were strengthened and fortified by a sacrifice duly performed and offered to them. Also, by strengthening the gods the sacrifices ensured that the seasons followed their proper sequence. It is only when Tishtrya is invoked in the sacrifice that the drought is defeated; only then can the rains give life to the world. The outcome of the cosmic battle between the forces of life and death depends on man's faithful observance of his ritual obligations.

Anahita, the Strong Undefiled Waters

It is natural that many religions should imagine the source of life and fruitfulness in female form. In Persia the goddess Ardvi Sura Anahita, the strong undefiled waters, is the source of all waters upon earth. She is the source of all fertility, purifying the seed of all males, sanctifying the womb of all females and purifying the milk in the mother's breast. From her heavenly home she is the source of the cosmic ocean. She is described as strong and bright, tall and beautiful, pure and nobly born. As befits her noble birth she wears a golden crown with eight rays and a hundred stars, a golden mantle and a golden necklace around her beautiful neck.

Such vivid details suggest that from early times statues were used in her worship. Certainly they were part of her cult from the time of Artaxerxes Mnemon, for an ancient Greek historian (Berossus) records that the King of Kings erected statues of her in cities as far apart as Babylon, Damascus, Ecbatana, Sardis and Susa. She became a popular deity in many lands. In Armenia she was described as 'the glory and life of Armenia, the giver of life, the mother of all wisdom, the benefactress of the entire human race, the daughter of the great and mighty Aramazda (Ahura Mazda)'. (Agathangelus, quoted by Gray, *Foundations, p. 59.*) She had many temples in Anatolia where

A bronze Parthian statue of a fertility goddess, probably Anahita, Lady and Source of the Waters.

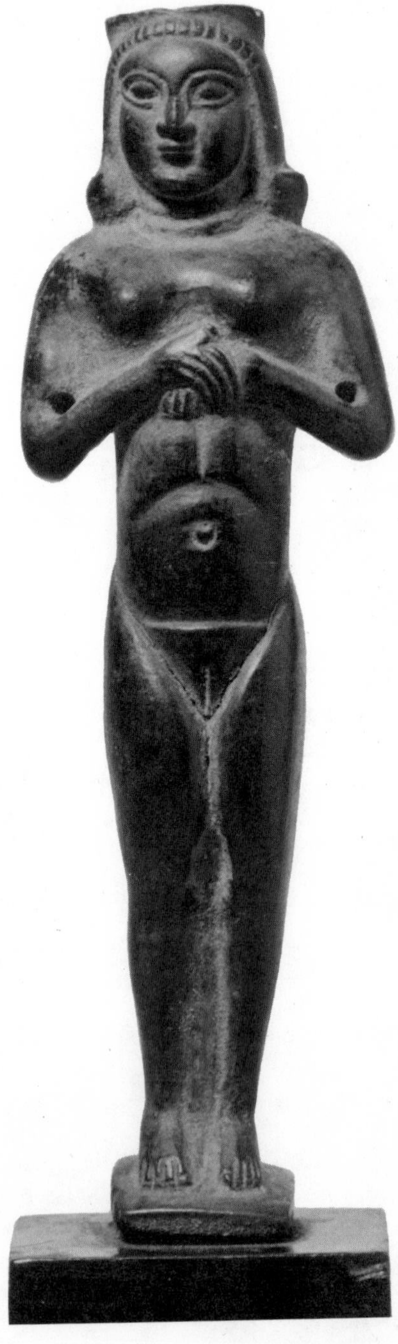

the Roman historian Strabo says the daughters of noble families were required to practise sacred prostitution at her shrine before marriage. It is difficult to say whether or not this was practised in Persia. All the religious texts condemn prostitution in the strongest possible terms, but it has been suggested that these condemnations arose because just such a practice existed. It would be completely wrong, however, to suggest there was an orgiastic cult around the lady of the waters, for we hear of priestesses who served her taking a vow of chastity. In Persia she was, and still is, an object of deep veneration, the source of life and the object of deeply felt gratitude.

Verethraghna, Victory

Whereas Vayu and Tishtrya are associated with natural phenomena, and Anahita is thought of in personal and loving terms, Verethraghna is an abstraction, or the personification of an idea. He is the expression of the aggressive, irresistible force of victory. In the hymn dedicated to him, *Yasht 14,* Verethraghna is said to have ten incarnations or forms, each form expressing the dynamic force of the god. The first incarnation is that of a strong wind; the second is the shape of a bull with yellow ears and golden horns; the third is that

A fifth- or sixth-century silver vase from Persia with a relief of a priestess of Anahita, an illustration which raises the question of the practice of temple prostitution. In Cappadocia the daughters of high-ranking people served in the temples of Anahita before marriage. We do not know if this was practised in Persia.

of a white horse with golden trappings; the fourth that of a burden-bearing camel, sharp-toothed, stamping forward; the fifth form is that of a boar, a sharp-toothed male boar that kills at one stroke, both wrathful and strong; the sixth is that of a youth at the ideal age of fifteen; the seventh the form of a swift bird, perhaps a raven; the eighth a wild ram; the ninth that of a fighting buck, and finally, the tenth is the form of a man holding a sword with a golden blade.

The similarity between the forms of Verethraghna and Tishtrya, who both appear as man, bull and horse is obvious. How is it that in Persian thought the gods can take different forms? As we shall see in more detail later (p. 57), the Zoroastrians believe that everything in the spiritual (*menog*) world has the faculty for possessing a material or *getig* form. This, they believe, is how the world came to be; it was the assumption of material form by the spiritual world. But whereas terrestial beings 'materialise under the form appropriate to their nature', heavenly or divine beings can 'materialise' under various forms–hence the three forms of Tishtrya and the ten of Verethraghna.

Unlike his Indian counterpart, Indra, or his Armenian counterpart Varhagn, the Persian Verethraghna has no myth in which he is said to defeat a monster or dragon. Instead he defeats 'the malice of men and demons' administering punishment to the untruthful and wicked. He is the strongest in strength, the most victorious in victory, the most glorious in glory. If he is offered sacrifice in the right way he gives victory in life and battle. If he is worshipped properly neither hostile armies nor plague will enter the Aryan countries. Verethraghna, then, represents an irresistible force. He is essentially a warrior god.

Two of his incarnations are particularly popular, that as a great bird and that as a boar. Ancient Persians viewed a raven's feathers with superstitious awe:

On this relief from Nimrud Dag in Commagene King Antiochus is shown shaking hands with Mithra. Whereas Herakles-Verethragna is portrayed in Greek fashion, naked, Mithra-Apollo is portrayed in typically Persian dress with cloak and leggings.

right *Detail of king Antiochus.*

far right *Detail of Mithra.*

The kingdom of Commagene was a buffer state between the Hellenic west and the Persian east. In political and religious affairs her kings sought a diplomatic union of the two traditions. The gods were, therefore, given both Greek and Persian names. On this relief from Arsameia in Commagene king Mithradates Kallinikos (a name mixing Persian and Greek elements) is shaking hands with a god named in an inscription as Herakles-Verethragna. Some scholars have incorrectly identified this king as Antiochus, and mistakenly located the relief at Nimrud Dag in Commagene.

they were thought to make a man inviolable and to bring him prosperity and glory. It may be that the raven which accompanies Mithras on the Roman monuments was originally intended as a symbol of the god Victory accompanying or assisting Mithras.

Certainly Verethraghna is said to accompany Mithra in his other form as a boar, a particularly appropriate symbol for the aggressive force of victory. In the ancient hymn to Mithra, *Yasht 10*, Verethraghna is pictured flying in front of Mithra:

in the shape of a wild, aggressive, male boar with sharp fangs
and sharp tusks, a boar that kills at one blow . . . has iron hind
feet, iron fore-feet, iron tendons, an iron tail, and iron jaws.

On all his opponents he inflicts a gory end:

he cuts to pieces everything at once, mingling together
on the ground the bones, the hair, the brains, and the blood
of men false to the contract.
Yt. 10:70–72, AHM. pp. 107ff

It is not surprising that Verethraghna was particularly popular among soldiers, and it may have been they who carried his worship so far and wide. He lies behind the figure of Herakles at Commagene, Vahaga in Armenia, Varlagn among the Saka, Vasaga in Sogdia and Artagn in Chorasmia. He is represented on Indo-Scythian coins and perhaps, as we have seen, on Mithraic monuments.

Rapithwin, Lord of the Noon-day Heat

Rapithwin is the lord of the noon-day heat and of the summer months, the necessary beneficial contrast to Tishtrya. When the sun stood still over the world before the entry of evil it stood at the station of Rapithwin. He is, then, lord of the ideal world. In Zoroastrian belief it was at the time of day belonging to Rapithwin that Ahura Mazda performed the sacrifice which produced creation. Equally at the end of time it will be at the time of Rapithwin that the resurrection of the dead will be completed. Thus he is not only lord of the primeval time, but also of the renovation. He is also active year by year: each time the demon of winter invades the world Rapithwin retreats beneath the earth and keeps the subterranean waters warm so that the plants and trees do not die. His annual return to earth in spring is a foreshadowing of that final triumph of good over which he will preside. The time when evil will be ultimately defeated and God's rule on earth will be made manifest . . .

is like the year, in which at springtime the trees have been made to blossom . . .
like the resurrection of the dead, new leaves are made to shoot from dry plants
and trees, and springtimes are made to blossom.
Z.S.xxxiv, 0+27, M.B.R.p.203

The feast of Rapithwin is part of the festival of Nauroz, the new day both of the actual year and of the future ideal time. His coming to earth is a time of joy and eschatological hope, a symbol of the final abiding triumph of the Good Creation.

Summary

Already we have seen something of the different characters of the ancient Persian gods. Some, such as Vayu, clearly belong to the Indo-Iranian tradition; with others, such as Rapithwin, we cannot be sure. While some, like Verethraghna, represent abstract concepts others, such as Tishtrya, represent natural phenomena. Some, such as Anahita, are described in anthropomorphic language, others, like Rapithwin, are not. Although there is no hint of a cosmic battle in the myth surrounding Anahita it is very much in evidence in the myth concerning Tishtrya. There is, then, a great diversity in the concepts of the various gods.

So far little has been said of the gods of the cult. With virtually all religious traditions the ritual is the centre of the religious life, and so we turn now to the ancient Persian gods concerned with the cult.

This wood-carving from south India shows the god Agni, fire, an ancient Indo-Iranian figure who appears in Persia as Atar. The fire was thought of as the meeting place between god and man, for it is on to the fire that the offerings of melted butter are poured, and it is at the fire that the gods receive the oblation. Thus the fire is the mediator between god and man. Agni is also, however, a god enthroned on high.

The Gods of the Cult

Atar, Fire

To this day the fire remains the centre of Hindu and Zoroastrian ritual, but its origins date right back to the Indo-European period. In India fire is revered under the name of Agni, and is at once both earthly and divine. As sacrifices are poured on to the fire, it is thought of as a mediator between man and the gods, for it is at this point that the two worlds are brought together. Agni is the god who, as fire, receives the sacrifice and as priest offers it to the gods. The element of fire also pervades the whole universe: the sun, in highest heaven, is kindled in the storm cloud and comes down to earth as lightning where he is ever reborn by the hands of men. Agni, therefore, is described as the path to the gods, through whom the summits of heaven may be reached.

The centrality of the fire in Zoroastrianism is perhaps one of the best known, and most misinterpreted, aspects of the faith. Pre-Zoroastrian though both belief and practices are, they have become thoroughly Zoroastrianised and it is often difficult in Persian mythology to separate the early from the later ideas. Fire is the son of Ahura Mazda, the visible sign of his presence, a symbol of his true order. One modern Parsi writes:

What, indeed, can be a more natural and more sublime representation of Him, who is Himself Eternal Light, than a pure, undefiled flame?
Masani, p. 80

The Zoroastrian ritual, however, preserves many of the ancient ideas. There the Fire is addressed directly and the priest presents offerings to it. In the litany to the Fire the priest chants the words:

I bless the sacrifice and prayer, the good offering, and the
wished-for offering, and the devotional offering (offered)
unto thee, O Fire! son of Ahura Mazda.
Worthy of sacrifice art thou, worthy of prayer,
Worthy of sacrifice mayest thou be, worthy of prayer,
In the dwellings of men.
Happiness may there be unto that man
Who verily shall sacrifice unto Thee.
Dhalla, Nyaishes, p. 155

In modern Zoroastrianism the fire is so holy that neither the sun's rays nor the eyes of an unbeliever must be allowed to see it. This may not always have been the case, for in ancient times fire altars were erected on mountain tops.

Very few myths about Atar have come down to us, though the early Christians seem to have known of more. One myth in the ancient hymn, the *Zamyad Yasht*, tells of the struggle between Atar and the monster Azhi Dahaka (Dahak) over the Divine Glory. Azhi, three-mouthed and of evil law, the embodiment of the destructive desire, rushed to grasp the Divine Glory so that he might extinguish it. Atar also rushed to grasp and save that unattainable Glory but Azhi, charging behind, 'blasphemies outpouring', roared that if Atar seized the glory he would rush on him and stop him from ever blazing forth on earth again. As Atar hesitated, Azhi rushed on to seize the glory. This time it was Atar's turn to utter threats. He warned Dahaka, 'get back you three-mouthed monster, if you seize the unattainable glory I shall flame up your bottom and blaze through your mouth so that you will never again advance upon the Ahura created earth'. (*Yt. 19: 59, based on Wolff*) Terrified, Azhi in his turn drew back, and the Divine Glory remained unattainable.

What the original significance of the myth was it is hard to say, but it does show once more that the ancient Persians saw life as a battle between the forces of good and evil. Atar, naturally, fought on behalf of the good, so that in one of the Zoroastrian prayers he is called 'the bold, good warrior'. The ancient association of Fire with the natural element comes out in another late text where, as lightning, he defeats the demon who seeks to delay the rains. These myths, however, no longer play a significant part in the faith of the Zoroastrians where, as we have seen, the Fire is the symbol of Ahura Mazda and the

Athsho, two Kushana representations of the Persian Atar, Fire. The fire on the shoulders is probably derived from Indian imagery of Agni. On the second coin Athsho carries tongues and hammer, tools for the kindling and preservation of the fire.

centre of their daily devotions. The Fire, is, however, still called on as a 'warrior' for the most sacred of fires, the Bahram Fire (see p. 125) is required to do battle, not with demons of drought, but with the spiritual demons of darkness.

Haoma, Plant and God

The Indo-Iranian Haoma (Soma in India) is a concept at once almost incomprehensible and yet strikingly familiar to the western mind. Haoma is both plant and god. The ritual pressing of the plant is likened to a number of celestial phenomena, the shining of the sun and the coming of the rains, yet he is also thought of as the divine priest who is himself the victim of a bloodless sacrifice, but who makes the blood sacrifice. From his death comes the defeat of evil and for the faithful life through sharing in a communion meal.

Soma is one of the main figures of Vedic ritual, where he appears also as both plant and god. The juice from the pressed plant is strained through a woollen filter into vats containing milk and water. The yellow liquid is likened to the rays of the sun and the flowing liquid to the pouring rain. Soma is therefore called the Lord or King of streams and the bestower of fertility. Since the drink is thought to have medicinal power the god is said to make the blind see and the lame walk. A being of universal dominion, he gives strength to the other gods among whom he acts as priest. He is also a great fighter and the priests who drink Soma are able to slay at a glance. The plant is found on the mountains, but the celestial being, purified in heaven, stands above all the worlds.

The Persian Haoma is very similar. The plant is now identified as ephedra. It is thought to give strength and healing in its natural state and much more so when it has been consecrated. The first four men said to have pressed haoma each received the boon of a great son, Vivanghvant who had Yima, Athwya who had Thraetaona, Thrita who had Keresaspa and Pourushaspa who had Zoroaster.

As Soma is a great fighter so Haoma is a great warrior:
Haoma killed the horned dragon
who, horse-devourer, men-devourer,
yellow and poisonous, had yellow poison
mounting on him to the height of a spear.
Gershevitch, IL. p. 63

In an ancient text recited during the sacrifice Haoma is besought to hurl his mace against the dragon, murderers, tyrants and harlots.

The celestial Haoma, the son of Ahura Mazda, is also the divine priest. He makes offerings to the other gods and, like earthly priests, must receive his portion of any animal sacrifice. This enables him to care for the soul of the animal, and should it not be set aside, the animal will then accuse the sacrificer at the judgment. As he came to Zoroaster when he pressed the haoma, so it is thought that Haoma will be present at every offering of the faithful. Thus within the sacrifice of haoma Haoma is at once god, priest and victim. The idea of the god's death in the ritual is contained in an ancient Indian text which reads:

Soma is a god and they kill him in that they press him.
S.B. 3, 9, 4, 17. D-G, Symbols, p. 82

From the sacrificial death of the divine priest, then, comes life and strength for the faithful. Moreover, the haoma consecrated in the daily ritual is a symbol of the White Hom which at the renovation of the world will make all men immortal; it is, as it were, a foretaste of that elixir of immortality. Quite how ancient this particular belief is, we do not know.

Thus in the figure of Haoma we have the concept of a warrior against evil, the divine priest himself offered in the oblation so that men may have life, and the divine presence being manifest on earth in the consecrated plant which grows in its natural state on the mountains.

The Indian Yama, god of death, riding a buffalo on which he carries the souls of the deceased.

Summary

In Persian belief the gods are not remote beings but powers encountered directly in the ritual. The characters of Atar and Haoma also illustrate the vast difference between Eastern and Western concepts of deity. Although myths and anthropomorphic imagery are used of Atar and Haoma, they are not personalised in the way the Greeks imagined Zeus, the Jews picture Yahweh, or the Muslims describe Allah. Any similarities that occur between Persian and Christian ideas must not be allowed to cloud our vision. We are moving in a different world; Persian thought must not be viewed through Christian-coloured spectacles.

Despite these remarks the heroic character of the heavenly beings does exist and is a theme which has already been noted. This is a trait which almost all ancient religions possess. In Persia there are a number of divine heroes; the stories told of them at times verge almost on the legendary rather than the mythical plane, but to omit these figures would leave a gap in our picture of ancient Persian mythology.

The Divine Heroes

Yima

Yima is another figure from Indo-Iranian belief. Although the Indian and Persian traditions agree over a number of details the general character of Yima (Yama in India) is strikingly different.

The outstanding feature of the Vedic Yama is that he was the first of the immortals to choose a mortal destiny. 'To please the gods he chose death, to please his offspring he did not choose immortality' (*RV. 10.13.4.ZDT, p. 132*). By treading the path of death he showed men the way to the path of the immortals that they might dwell with him in his abode of song. As he was the king of the dead, death became known as the path of Yama, a picture which in time came to have a rather sinister colouring, as some rather fearsome statues show.

The Persian myths, for one reason or another, have suffered in the course of transmission and it is difficult to reconstruct the total picture. Yima is most revered in Persia for his thousand-years' rule over the earth, a rule characterised

A seventeenth-century illustration from the Shah name *depicting Yima (Jamshid) on his throne ruling over a world of peace and plenty.*

right *A scene from the* Shah name *showing the great king Takhmoruw defeating the demons.*

by peace and plenty, where demons with all their foul works–untruth, hunger, sickness and death–held no sway. The world was so prosperous under his rule that it had to be made larger on three occasions so that at the end of his reign it was twice as large as when he began. Yima thus stands as the ideal prototype of all kings, the model for all rulers to emulate. In Persia, as in India, he appears as a king rather than as a god.

Yima is also praised for his construction of a *vara,* or cavern. Warned by the creator that three terrible winters, which will destroy all men and animals, are to befall mankind, Yima constructed a vara into which he took the seeds of every kind of cattle, plant and the best of men. Although this belief bears some striking resemblances to the Semitic flood story the later Persian texts state that the purpose of the vara was to re-people the world after a winter which will occur at the close of history. As a similar myth occurs in Scandinavian belief it may be that the two traditions have preserved, in fossilised form, myths dating back thousands of years to the time of the Indo-Europeans.

But Yima is also remembered as a sinner. Zoroaster condemned him as one who sought to please men by giving them ox flesh to eat. In other texts he is said to have been proud and to have lied by claiming divine qualities. One ancient text relates that when he began to delight in falsehood his glory flew away from him three times in the shape of a bird. The first time it was caught by Mithra, the second by Thraetaona and the third by Keresaspa. Why it left him three times we do not know, though some have suggested that it represents the three-fold structure of society over which Yima had ruled–the priests, the warriors and the artisans. The precise nature of his sin is also in doubt. It has been conjectured that a bull sacrifice, which was thought to make men immortal, was associated with Yima, thus attributing to Yima the power truly belonging to God in Zoroaster's faith, the power to make men immortal. Whether this was the ancient belief we cannot really say, the later texts simply describe him as telling lies and claiming divine powers. Whatever his sin, with his glory gone Yima was left trembling in sorrow before his enemies.

The end of Yima in the Persian tradition is also something of a mystery. One old hymn says that he was cut in two by his brother, Spityura, but in later tradition it is the evil Dahak, pictured not as a mythical being but as a wicked

In this wood-carving from south India Indra is shown sitting on a hunting dog and holding his symbol of power. Indra is the most popular Vedic deity, being revered particularly as a warrior. His counterpart in Persia is the demon of heresy.

human tyrant (Zahhak), who kills Yima and takes over his earthly realm.

Despite his sin Yima is still thought to be a figure worthy of veneration. Persepolis, the site of the great Achaemenid palace, is popularly called the throne of Jamshid (the later form of Yima's name). Yima is also credited with instituting the great annual Persian festival, Nauroz, which is still an occasion for great merriment and the giving of presents.

Hoshang and Takhmoruw

In ancient Persia there seems to have been more than one tradition about the first king, for as well as Yima there are two other figures called the first kings, Hoshang and Takhmoruw. The texts as we have them fit these two 'first kings' into their scheme of myth and history simply by making them into successive primeval legendary rulers, although they were once more than this.

Hoshang was ruler of the seven regions in ancient times. He ruled over men and demons; before him all sorcerers and demons fled down to darkness. Mazana was thought to be Mazanderan, whose southern boundary is marked by Mount Demavend. It is the home of many demons and sorcerers, two-thirds of whom were slain by the valiant Hoshang. His reign saw the establishment of law on earth and from him and his wife rose the race of the Iranians.

Takhmoruw, like Hoshang and all goodly men, defeated the demons. He attacked idolatry, wizards and witches, and propagated the true reverence for the creator. In his fight against evil he is said to have transferred the Evil Spirit into the shape of a horse and ridden him round the earth for thirty years.

A fifth- or fourth-century BC gold amulet from the Oxus treasure, with winged and horned griffins.

Thrita, Thraetaona, Faridun

Religious traditions the world over preserve stories of battles between godly heroes and monsters. In ancient India the most famous of these is Indra, who destroyed Vritra the demon of drought with his mace, the thunderbolt, thus liberating the waters which give life to men. Another such hero is Trita, who is described in remarkably similar terms. Trita with his thunderbolt slew the three-headed, six-eyed serpent, Vrisvarupa. On another occasion Trita slew a demon in the shape of a boar with his mace. Trita roars with the storm and when he blows on them the flames of Agni rise up. But unlike Indra Trita is also remembered as a great preparer and drinker of the sacred soma.

In Persia the work of this god appears under two names, Thrita the healer and preparer of haoma, and Thraetaona (Faridun in the later texts), the one who slays the monster. Thrita was the third man who prepared haoma for the corporeal world. He prayed to the creator for a medicine that would withstand the pain, disease, rottenness, infection and death that the evil spirit was working among men by his witchcraft. In answer to Thrita's prayer the creator brought down the myriads of healing plants that grow round the Gaokerena tree in the cosmic ocean. Thrita is therefore remembered as the one who drove away sickness, fever and death from men.

Thraetaona is similarly invoked against the itch, fevers and incontinency, for all these are the work of the three-headed, three-jawed, six-eyed mighty dragon, Dahak, the lie demon whom the Evil Spirit created to slay righteousness and the settlements of men. Thraetaona is invoked against the work of Dahak for he is thought to have defeated the dragon in battle, a battle which took place in the Varena, or the heavens. Thraetaona clubbed the evil Dahak about the head, neck and heart but could not slay him. At last he took a sword and stabbed the monster whereupon a multitude of horrible creatures crept from his loathsome body. In fear of the world being filled with such vile creatures as snakes, toads, scorpions, lizards, tortoises and frogs, Thraetaona refrained from cutting the monster to pieces. Instead he bound and imprisoned him in Mount Demavend, an action that mankind will one day rue, as we shall see.

His victory over Dahak gave Thraetaona the rank of the most victorious of men, apart, of course, from Zoroaster. It is because of his victorious character that Thraetaona was able to seize the glory of Yima as it fled the fallen hero. Because he was triumphant over the violence of Dahak he is invoked by the faithful to repel all those who are violent.

Parthian amulet showing Faridun grasping a demon and about to slay him with his mace. The reverse of this shows an interesting example of a Roman symbol, the suckling wolf, in a Persian setting. How the Persians interpreted this figure we do not know.

A Persian wool carpet dating from the fourth or third century BC, the oldest knotted wool carpet known to the world. It was excavated in southern Siberia in 1949. The four-rayed star motif also appears on some Luristan bronzes. The outer borders show elks and mounted horsemen parading round the central pattern.

A fifth-century gold rhyton or drinking vessel with the body of a winged lion. The style of this rhyton is remarkably like that of other models found in different parts of the Persian empire. The unity of the styles may suggest a distinct school of art. The care lavished on these treasures is well illustrated by the fact that about 136 feet of single-strand wire was twisted to decorate the lip of a similar rhyton from Hamadan-Ecbatana.

A gold plaque from the Oxus treasure showing a Mede carrying a bundle of barsom. The Oxus treasure, found by local peasants in 1877, appears to consist of votive offerings to a temple.

Keresaspa

Keresaspa, the youthful hero who wore sidelocks and carried a club is another great dragon-slaying hero of ancient Persia. Like Faridun he is not recognised as a god, and so a Zoroastrian cannot pray to him, but only offer a sacrifice with a special intention for him. There were many myths, or perhaps we should call them legends, about this great adventurer, but they only exist now in fragmentary form. He is said to have defeated the 'golden-heeled' monster, Gandarewa, who rushed with open jaws to devour, whose head rose to the sun and who would devour twelve men at once. The battle with this awesome monster is said to have lasted for nine days and nights in the cosmic ocean.

Many are the monsters, highwaymen and murderers who have fallen to Keresaspa. One example is the giant bird Kamak who hovered over the earth, and whose wingspread was so great that the rain could not fall. On one occasion Keresaspa was involved in a hair-raising escapade with

. . . the horned dragon
who, horse-devourer, men-devourer,
yellow and poisonous, had yellow poison
mounting on him to the height of a spear.
On the back of this dragon Keresaspa the hero
happened to stew his meat in a kettle
at lunch time.
The monster began to be hot and perspire;
he darted forth with a jolt
spilling the boiling water:
heroic Keresaspa fled in terror.
Ys. 9:11, Gershevitch, IL. p. 63

It was because of his courage that Keresaspa was able to catch the glory as it fled from Yima.

At the end of the world Keresaspa will once again save men from a monster, for Dahaka will break free from his prison in the mountain. With demonic fury he will attack creation, perpetrating horrific sins and devouring one-third of the men and animals. The creator will resurrect the brave Keresaspa, who will smite the monster with his famous club and kill him, so saving mankind.

Although Keresaspa is respected for his bravery, and though he may be invoked to repel the violence of robbers, he forever remains something of a doubtful character in the Zoroastrian tradition. He was a brave, but 'devil-may-care' hero, who lacked respect for the fire, the traditional centre of the religious life, and had little concern for the religion. When at death he prayed to enter heaven, although he recounted his deeds the creator rejected him. It was only after many pleas from the weeping Keresaspa, the weeping angels, Zoroaster and the animal world that he was finally admitted.

The stories surrounding Keresaspa are good examples of the narrow line which can divide myth from legend. Although they now exist in legendary rather than mythical form, the association of Keresaspa with the end of the world may suggest that these stories once had a greater religious significance than they have now. As with many figures from the ancient lore of different nations he is remembered for his bravery, not for his misdeeds.

Summary of the Ancient Mythology

Although the ancient 'pagan' Persian belief has been preserved only in the Zoroastrian and Indian traditions, not in its own right, we can still reconstruct a great deal of the earliest Persian mythology. The ancient picture of the universe was of a flat, peaceful earth, where originally there was no evil of any kind. This state of tranquillity was shattered by the intrusion of evil which afflicted terrestial as well as cosmic life.

As one might expect from an ancient nomadic people, the myths of the Indo-Iranians often centred on battles seen in and reflected by nature. The drought and the rains, the thunderstorm and the heat of the sun, all reflected cosmic encounters to the ancient Persians. Yet this ancient mythology cannot

A plaque from a quiver at Luristan. Speculation has been rife over the identification of the figures. It has been argued that the identical pair of gods at the top are the divine pair, Mitra-Varuna, and represent the sky, the bull on the right of the picture is said to represent the cosmic bull slain by Mithra. The figure in the middle register, standing between two lions, is said to be Indra representing the atmosphere, while the lower register is thought to show the gods of the productive workers. These identifications, though ingenious, are by no means certain.

be described simply as a form of nature worship: some of the gods represent completely abstract ideas such as victory, and while some gods are described in human terms, others are not.

To the ancient Persian the divine was not a distant reality far removed from human experience but a factor of everyday life. Religion was something celebrated on mountains and not in confined temples. The gods pervaded the universe; thus Atar, the son of God, is present in the heavens, in the atmosphere and in the humble household fire. Man's daily and ritual life involves direct and immediate contact with the divine beings. The rituals were made up not only of hymns sung to distant beings–the sky, sun and stars–but also of hymns chanted to forces present in the fire and the haoma–hymns to Fire and Haoma.

Ancient Persian mythology was concerned not only with cosmic battles, abstract concepts and ritual figures, but also with fabulous heroes, the model of kingship, the brave hero, the original medicine man. All these views of man, society, the world and the divine are expressed in ancient myths preserved by the Zoroastrians and in some cases by the Hindus. That we are able to reconstruct the beliefs of thousands of years ago is due to the intensely conservative nature of the two religious traditions.

above *Luristan, in south-west Iran, high in the Zagros mountains, produced an ancient civilisation famous for its metalwork. It was subject to many sources of influence and the identification of figures on the pins, bronzes, amulets and cultic standards, presents a major problem. As on this pin the deities are frequently associated with monsters.*

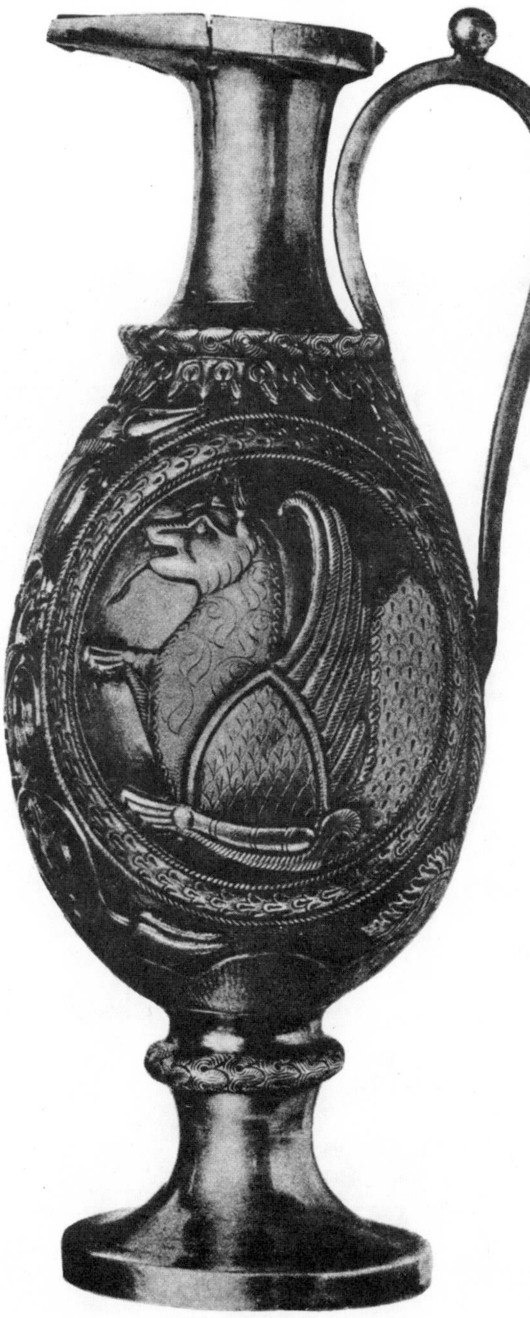

left *The figure on this silver ewer is that of Senmurw, a mythological dragon-peacock, who often figures in Sasanian art.*

A fire-temple on a hill top near Isfahan. Zoroastrianism still retains something of the ancient Persian tradition of a religion practised in the mountains.

ZOROASTRIAN MYTHOLOGY

Conflict between Gods and Demons

Dualism, the belief that there are two fundamentally opposed forces at work in the universe, is a characteristically Zoroastrian doctrine. The ancient Aryans believed in the two opposing forces of Truth or Order (Asha) and the Lie or Disorder, an idea that was taken up and developed in Zoroastrianism where the faithful are called the followers of Truth, *ashavans,* and the wicked the followers of the lie, *drugvans.*

In his hymns Zoroaster appears to assume that his hearers would be acquainted with a myth in which this dualism is cast into the form of two opposing spirits, for he says:

I will speak of the two spirits
Of whom the holier said unto the destroyer at the beginning of existence:
'Neither our thoughts nor our doctrines nor our minds' forces,
Neither our choices nor our words nor our deeds,
Neither our consciences nor our souls agree.'
Ys. 45:2, D-G, Hymns, p. 93

This idea of the opposition of two forces was so developed in later Zoroastrianism that two distinct vocabularies were used. Thus when Zoroastrians refer to the forces of good they speak of the head, the hand, speaking and dying, but when they refer to a member of the evil forces they speak of the skull, the claw, howling and perishing.

We have already noted that to the Zoroastrians there can be no greater sin than to associate good with evil, that is, to suggest that the good world is the creation of the Evil Spirit. The opposite applies equally forcefully: there can be no greater sin than to associate God with evil. Good and evil are contrary realities, as are darkness and light, or life and death. They are opposing substances, not simply different aspects of the same reality. Evil is not simply the absence of good, it is a real substance and force. Good and evil cannot co-exist, they are mutually destructive and must ultimately derive from two first causes which are themselves mutually antagonistic and irreconcileable. The opposition of good and evil, or God and the devil, to use Christian terms, is the basis of all Zoroastrian mythology, theology and philosophy. To see how they are worked out we will look first at the Zoroastrians' concept of the divine and the demonic forces and then at their myths.

The Forces of Good

Ahura Mazda, the Wise Lord

Ahura Mazda (Ohrmazd in later texts), meaning the Wise Lord, is the name given to God by the Zoroastrians. As his name implies, he is characterised by wisdom–undeceived and undeceiving, the Lord is bounteous and perfect goodness. The mother and father of creation, he made the paths of the sun, moon and stars. He was, is and will be, in other words he is eternal, but at the present time he is not omnipotent for he is limited by his arch-enemy, the Evil Spirit. The time will come, however, when evil will be overcome and Ahura Mazda will reign omnipotent.

The terms in which Ohrmazd is described are often naturalistic. He wears a star-decked robe. His fairest forms are the sun on high and the light on earth; the 'swift-horsed sun' is said to be his eye. His throne is in the highest heaven, in celestial light. There he holds court, and ministering angels carry out his commands. Although this symbolism may have been taken literally by many, this must not be supposed to be the case for all Zoroastrians. Much of the mythology has, as we shall see, an abstract character.

To a Zoroastrian Ohrmazd is above all perfect goodness–he has no association with evil. Zoroastrians condemn the Christian god as evil for he allows his creation, and even his own son, to suffer. Suffering is regarded as evil for it spoils the Good Creation; it is something that God cannot yet control, but which he will one day defeat. God is the source of all that is good: light, life, beauty, joy, health. He is the power behind every throne, the inspiration of all that is true and whose earthly symbol is the righteous man.

The Kushana Ashaeixsho, Persian Asha Vahista or the Best Truth, the third of the Amesha Spentas. He is shown with a radiate nimbus, holding out his hand, perhaps in blessing.

The Amesha Spentas, Sons and Daughters of God

Zoroaster spoke of seven beings or 'aspects' of God which he had created by an act of will. They are Spenta Mainyu, Vohu Manah, Asha, Kshathra Vairya, Armaiti, Haurvatat and Ameretat, or to give them their English form, the Bounteous Spirit, the Good Mind, Truth, the Desired Kingdom, Devotion, Integrity and Immortality. The essential characteristic of God is the Bounteous or Creative Spirit. This belongs to God alone but the other aspects are facets of God in which man can share: they are the means by which God approaches man and man approaches God. So Zoroaster declares that whoever gives heed to Ahura Mazda and obeys him will attain Integrity and Immortality through the deeds of the Good Mind (*Ys.* 45: 5). It is through the Good Mind that men follow the paths of Truth, gain Integrity and Immortality and thereby attain the Kingdom. Man can thus share in the nature of God; indeed, his religious duty is to be united with his ultimate source or creator.

There has been much scholarly debate over the origin of these 'aspects'. Some believe that the figures are based on ancient gods, but whatever their source what matters most is an appreciation of the high ideals and the profound thought that they embody. In later Zoroastrianism much more picture imagery is used in association with these figures, who have been compared with the archangels of Christianity. Ahura Mazda came to be identified with the Creative Spirit, and the figure of Sraosha is brought in to make up the seven-fold structure of the divine 'hierarchy'. All seven sit on golden thrones beside Ahura Mazda in their abode the House of Song, the haven to which the righteous pass at death. Each of the 'Immortals' protects a part of creation: Vohu Manah protects animals, Asha the fire, Kshathra the metals, Armaiti the earth, Ameretat the plants and Haurvatat the water. Man stands under the protection of Ahura Mazda himself. The Immortals all play such an important part in Zoroastrian belief that each of them is worth looking at individually.

Despite the Roman military dress – mailed skirt, cuirass and crested helmet – this is the Kushana deity Shaoreoro, probably a form of the Persian Kshathra Vairya, Desirable Kingdom. This warrior imagery is particularly appropriate, for the kingdom is symbolised by metals and is to be established on earth when the battle with evil has been won.

Vohu Manah, Good Mind

Vohu Manah, the first-born of God, sits at the right hand of Ahura Mazda and acts almost as adviser. Although he protects useful animals in the world he

On this relief from an archway at Persepolis the winged symbol of Ahura Mazda hovers above the king of kings. The Achaemenids do not appear to have represented god in human form, rather they used this symbol based on Babylonian and Egyptian models. The king, the earthly representative of God, towered over other men in his regal glory.

nevertheless deals with men as well. It was Vohu Manah who appeared visibly to Zoroaster, and it is he who keeps a daily record of men's thoughts, words and deeds. At death the righteous soul is greeted by Vohu Manah and led by him to the highest heaven. Behind this picture imagery still lies the belief in the Good Mind as the personification of God's wisdom, working in man and leading man to God, for it is through the Good Mind that the knowledge of the Good Religion is attained. The demons to whom he is opposed are Aeshma (Wrath) and Az (Wrong Mindedness), but above all, Akah Manah (Vile Thoughts or Discord).

Asha, Truth

Asha, the most beautiful of the Immortals, represents not only the opposite of untruth, but also the divine law and moral order in the world. The believer is called an *ashavan,* a follower of Asha. Those who do not know Asha forfeit heaven, for they are outside the whole order of God. The righteous pray that they might see this heavenly sovereign so that they might follow his paths and dwell in his joyous paradise. Asha preserves order on earth for he smites disease, death, fiends, sorcerers and vile creatures–all who contravene the order of the world which God wills. Asha even preserves order in hell, by seeing that the demons do not punish the wicked more than they deserve. His chief opponent is Indra, who represents the Spirit of Apostasy, for apostasy is that which draws men away from the law and order of God.

Kshathra Vairya, the Desired Kingdom

In many ways Kshathra Vairya is the most abstract of the immortals. He is the personification of God's might, majesty, dominion and power. In the celestial world this represents the kingdom of heaven, and on earth that kingdom which establishes God's will on earth by helping the poor and weak and by overcoming all evil. Because of his protection of metals he is associated with the stream of molten metal that will test all men at the end of the world. It is said, therefore, that through him God allots final rewards and punishments. His particular opponent is Saura, the arch-demon of Misgovernment, Anarchy and Drunkenness.

The figure on this Kushana coin has been identified by a number of scholars as Vohu Manah. Sitting on a throne and holding a sceptre and diadem, the figure is one of regal power.

Armaiti, Devotion

Armaiti is the daughter of Ahura Mazda and sits at his left hand. As she presides over the earth she is said to give pasture to the cattle, but her true character is displayed by her name, which means Fit-mindedness, or Devotion. She is the personification of faithful obedience, religious harmony and worship. She is said to have appeared visibly to Zoroaster, an appropriate piece of symbolism in view of the prophet's faithful obedience to his call and his deep spirit of devotion. Armaiti is distressed when robbers, evil men and disrespectful wives walk free, but she rejoices when the righteous cultivate the land and rear cattle, or when a righteous son is born. Her particular opponents are Taromaiti (Presumption) and Pairimaiti (Crooked-Mindedness).

Ardoxsho, a Kushana figure who has been identified as either Ashi-Oxsho, the genius of Fate or Recompense, the daughter of Ahura Mazda and sister of Mithra, Sraoṣha and Rashnu; or as Ardvi Vaxsha, a local eastern Persian goddess of water and moisture, related to the great Ardvi Sura Anahita.

Haurvatat and Ameretat, Integrity and Immortality

Since these two feminine beings are always mentioned together in the texts, they are dealt with together here. Haurvatat, meaning wholeness, totality or fullness (often translated as Integrity), is the personification of what salvation means to the individual. Ameretat (literally deathlessness) is the other aspect of salvation, immortality. They are associated with water and vegetation, their gifts are wealth and herds of cattle, so that they represent the ideals of vigour, the sources of life and growth. Their particular opponents are Hunger and Thirst.

Sraosha, Obedience

Sraosha, Obedience or Discipline, is one of the most popular figures in Zoroastrianism. The god is present at every divine ceremony, for he is embodied in men's prayers and hymns, and as god conveys the prayers to heaven. He is invoked in his hymn as the 'holy ritual chief'. As the Zoroastrian ritual is a potent force which destroys evil, so Sraosha is described as a warrior in armour, the best smiter of the Lie. With his battle axe he smashes the skulls of demons and hews down Angra Mainyu, but he is opposed above all to Aeshma (Fury). 'Obedience', the embodiment of the sacred word, is the victorious force in the constant battle against the destructive forces of evil. The abstract quality of the figure is obvious, but it is not denuded of mythical imagery. Thus Sraosha protects the world at night when the demons are on the prowl. He was the first to chant the *Gathas,* to spread the sacred ritual twigs, the barsom, and to offer prayer to Ahura Mazda. His house, with its thousand pillars, is on the highest peak of Mount Haraiti. It is self-lit within, and lit by the stars without. He is drawn from there in his chariot by four beautiful white horses with swift golden feet. It is he who greets and watches over the soul at death. With Mithra and Rashnu he presides over the judgment of the soul (see p. 62).

The mythical imagery brings out very clearly the Zoroastrian understanding of the ritual, the stress on obedience to the divine word, obedience as the embodiment of the divine word, ritual and obedience as forces which preserve the soul and ultimately determine its fate. Obedience is not thought of as a passive quality in Zoroastrianism but rather as an active force, victorious in the fight with evil.

This is very much the picture of 'obedience' which appears in the *Gathas.* Zoroaster offers his life to God and to truth, together with his good thoughts, words and deeds, obedience and power. Similarly, obedience aportions the rewards at the end. At the outcome, at the attaining of the straight paths to Ahura Mazda, it is 'obedience' that is supreme. Scholars argue over the ambiguity of 'obedience' in the *Gathas,* whether it is simply an abstract concept or a god, but perhaps Zoroaster intended the ambiguity. The later Pahlavi books may not have distorted the prophet's teaching as violently as many believe when they made Sraosha one of the Immortals.

The figure on this pin from Luristan has been identified as Sraosha, the god of obedience. The cocks' heads on the pin do suggest the association of Sraosha with the bird, but the identification of this, and many other Luristan bronzes, is rather speculative.

The Yazatas, or Worshipful Ones

The Immortals are not the only heavenly beings in Zoroastrianism. There are also the Yazatas, the adorable or worshipful ones. In the heavenly council the Yazatas rank third in importance after Ahura Mazda and the Immortals. Although in theory they are innumerable, certain figures naturally dominate, mainly those who have a particular day of the month assigned to them in the Zoroastrian calendar. The most important of them, such as Mithra or Anahita, usually have a hymn or *Yasht* of their own. Since the main Yazatas, Vayu, Anahita, Haoma, Atar, Verethraghna, Rapithwin and Mithra, are dealt with elsewhere in this book there is little point in giving a complete catalogue here. Instead it will be useful to look at them as a group. On the whole they tend to be either the guardian spirits of the sun, moon, stars etc., or the personifications of such abstract ideas as blessing, truth or peace. It would be wrong, at least in the case of modern Zoroastrianism, to regard the religion as polytheistic and the Yazatas as gods of a pantheon like the figures of ancient Greek mythology. Zoroastrians believe that Ohrmazd is too great, too exalted for men to trouble him with their small petitions, penances or offerings. Instead they choose their own personal protector whom they approach. This does not mean that they do not revere or praise the love, power and sovereignty of Ahura Mazda, any more than a Roman Catholic loses sight of the love of God in seeking the aid and comfort of a saint. The Parsis, therefore, justifiably claim that the true parallel to the Yazatas are not the gods of 'pagan' pantheons, but the saints or angels of Christianity.

These then are the beings of the heavenly world in Zoroastrian belief. In short, Zoroastrians believe in one ultimate God or power, Ahura Mazda, who is absolute goodness, wisdom and knowledge, whose being man can share by partaking of the different aspects of his character, by following the path of Good Mind and Truth. His will is administered in detail by a number of 'ministering angels' who themselves are objects of love and devotion for the faithful, although none can ever replace the Wise Lord.

Opposed to the heavenly court is the world of the Evil Spirit, and it is to that we now turn.

The Kaba of Zoroaster which faces the royal tombs at Naqsh-i Rustam. It stands some thirty feet high. Many believe that it was an ancient place of worship, but there is little evidence to support this.

The Forces of Evil

Although the Persian texts leave the reader in no doubt about the horrible and vile nature of the demonic world, it is rarely described in such clear terms as the heavenly world. The arch-demons are not fitted into such a neat system as the archangels are and we are only able to reconstruct the pattern of their hierarchy because they are paired off with the heavenly beings at the end of the world. This lack of system may not be unintentional, since one of the chief characteristics of evil is its disorder and disunity.

Angra Mainyu

Angra Mainyu, or Ahriman as his name appears in the Middle Persian dialect, is the leader of the demonic hordes. Although his name does not occur as a personal name in the *Gathas,* the compound does appear and the idea of the 'Wicked One' is much in evidence. His aim is the ruin and destruction of the world. He dwells in the 'abode of wickedness' or of 'Worst Thought' and the *daevas* are said to be the 'Progeny of Evil Purpose'. Since the *Gathas* here, as elsewhere, depict figures in abstract form one has to turn to the later texts for the mythological descriptions. He is the demon of demons, and dwells in an abyss of endless darkness in the north, the traditional home of the demons. Ignorance, harmfulness and disorder are the characteristics of Ahriman. He can change his outward form and appear as a lizard, a snake or a youth. His aim is always to destroy the creation of Ohrmazd, and to this end he follows behind the creator's work, seeking to spoil it. As Ohrmazd creates life, Ahriman creates death; for health he produces disease, for beauty, ugliness. All man's ills are due entirely to Ahriman. The birth of Zoroaster was a great blow to the Evil Spirit, who tried to seduce the prophet into evil, without success. At the end of the world, despite all his efforts, it is he who will be defeated and his miscreation annihilated. It is interesting that the later texts state that the Evil Spirit has no material form. The idea appears to be that as the material world is the creation of God it must necessarily be good. Since good and evil cannot co-exist it follows that the Evil Spirit can have no material form, he can only reside like a parasite in the bodies of men and animals, and this cannot be said to be a true material existence.

Aeshma, Fury

Aeshma is the demon of wrath, fury and outrage, the personification of brutality, constantly seeking to stir up strife and war. When he fails to produce evil for the Good Creation, then he turns his attention to the Evil Creation and stirs up strife in the camp of the demons. In his assaults on men he is particularly aided by the tongues of the wicked, for they stir up anger and wrath. He accompanies those influenced by intoxicants and has as his offspring the demons of 'dishevelled hair'. His disruptive work in the world is held in check by Sraosha, the incarnation of religious obedience and devotion, the force which will ultimately rid the world of wrath.

Azhi Dahaka

The term Druj, Lie or Deceit, is often used as a designation for Angra Mainyu or for a particular fiend, or again for a class of demons the most notorious of whom is Azhi Dahaka, a figure we have met before (pp. 37, 43). Dahaka, with his three heads, six eyes and three jaws, is painted in clearer and more mythological colours than most of the demons. His body is full of lizards, scorpions and other vile creatures so that if he were cut open the whole world would be filled with such creates. On one occasion he offered in sacrifice to Anahita a hundred horses, a thousand oxen and ten thousand lambs, praying that he might be allowed to depopulate the earth–his constant desire. On another occasion he approached Vayu with sacrifice from his accursed palace with its

golden beams, throne and canopy, but his destructive desires were scorned by both of the heavenly beings.

Filled with the urge to destroy, this offspring of the Evil Spirit sought to extinguish the sacred flame, but was foiled by the hero Yima. He had his revenge, for he not only stole the daughters of the great ruler but also sawed Yima himself in two. The sweetness of his victory was short-lived however, for the hero Thraetaona liberated the maidens, and imprisoned Dahaka in Mount Demavend. Here he remains until the end of history when he will again attack the world, devour one third of its creatures and smite fire, water and vegetation until he is finally slain by the resurrected Keresaspa.

The Nature of Evil

These are the three demons most clearly described; of the others we know little but their names. Even from these small crumbs of evidence, however, we can obtain a fairly clear picture of the general character of evil and its manifestations. Among the demons are Jealousy, Arrogance, Lethargy, and Wrong-mindedness. One who is often mentioned is the Druj Nasu, the corpse demon, who is the personification of the spirit of corruption, decomposition, contagion and impurity. Another force of evil is Jahi, the demonic female embodiment of debauchery. The Yatus, magicians or sorcerers, are further manifestations of the disruptive forces of evil.

The total character of evil, then, is negative: its aims are to destroy, corrupt and deface. Its greatest work is to bring suffereing and death, the corruption and apparent destruction of God's chief creation, man. All that is horrible in man and the world, both physical and moral evil, is the work of Ahriman. The Zoroastrians do not have the theological problem of evil in the world which most monotheistic religions have to struggle with, namely, why does God allow suffering. The Zoroastrian answer is, he does not. Evil is a fact which God cannot at present control, but one day he will be victorious. History is the scene of the battle between the two forces. Let us now turn to the understanding of that history in the myths of creation, the death of the individual and the end of the world.

The Myth of Creation

Ohrmazd, dwelling on high in endless light, has no direct contact with the evil Ahriman in his deepest darkness, for between the two lies the void. The power of each, then, is limited by the other and both are spatially limited by the void. Ohrmazd is eternal, but Ahriman is not for he will one day be destroyed.

At first the two existed without coming into conflict. Although Ohrmazd in his omniscience knew of the Evil Spirit, Ahriman, ever ignorant and stupid, was not aware of the Wise Lord's existence. As soon as he saw Ohrmazd and the light his destructive nature prompted him to attack and to destroy. Ohrmazd offered him peace if he would only praise the Good Creation. But Ahriman, judging others by himself, believed that an offer of peace could only be made from a position of weakness, so he rejected the offer and sought to destroy that which he saw. Ohrmazd knew that if the battle were to last for ever Ahriman could, indeed, keep his threat, and suggested a fixed period for the battle. Ahriman, being slow-witted, agreed and thereby ensured his ultimate downfall. The point behind this idea seems to be that if evil is allowed to operate quietly, steadily and unobtrusively it can disrupt and destroy, but once it is drawn out into the open, engaged in battle and shown for what it is, it cannot succeed.

According to the orthodox tradition, history spans twelve thousand years. The first three thousand years is the period of the original creation; the second three thousand pass according to the will of Ohrmazd; the third three thousand is to be a period of the mixing of the wills of good and evil, and in the fourth period the Evil Spirit will be defeated. In the major Zoroastrian heresy, Zurvanism, the twelve thousand years are divided very differently, the first nine thousand years being the period of the rule of evil and the final three thousand the time of the defeat of evil. It may be that this second form was the older tradition.

After fixing the period for battle Ohrmazd recited the sacred prayer of Zoroastrianism, the *Ahuna Var*. On hearing this kernel of the Good Religion the Evil Spirit realised his inability to defeat the forces of good and fell back into hell where he lay unconscious for three thousand years.

Knowing that Ahriman would never change his destructive character, Ohrmazd began to create. Out of his very essence of light he produced the spiritual, or *menog*, form of the creatures. First he created the 'Immortals', then the Yazatas, and finally he began the creation of the universe: first the sky, then water, earth, the tree, the animal and, last of all, man. All these creations are completely independent of Ahriman. They are not reliant on him at all for their happiness, for Ohrmazd, unlike Ahriman, does not contemplate anything which he cannot achieve. The creatures belong entirely to God. Ohrmazd is both mother and father to creation: as mother he conceives the spiritual world and, it is said, as father he gives birth to it in material form. Ahriman in his turn creates, or rather miscreates, his own offspring from his evil nature, giving rise to all that is vile–wolves, frogs, whirlwinds, sandstorms, leprosy and so on.

The Zoroastrian creation myth is based on the ancient concept of the universe, but now it is Ohrmazd who creates the sky, which functions not only as a shell enclosing the world but also as a prison in which Ahriman is ensnared. When first produced the material creation was in an ideal state: the tree was without bark and thorn, the ox was white and shining like the moon and the archetypal man, Gayomart, was shining like the sun. This ideal state was shattered by the onslaught of Ahriman on the world. After he had fallen unconscious into hell

The bridegroom in procession to a traditional Parsi Zoroastrian wedding. Man has a religious duty to take a wife, have children and thereby increase the Good Religion. The author is heavily indebted to Professor Mary Boyce for her generous permission to use this and other original photographic material.

A Zoroastrian priest, Ervad Firoze Kotwal, sitting cross-legged in his white robes reciting the confessional.

the demons tried to arouse him with promises of how they would assault creation and inflict on it anguish and unhappiness, but all to no avail. Then came the wicked Jahi, the personification of all female impurity. She promised to afflict the holy man and the ox with so much suffering that life would not seem worth living. She also announced her intention of attacking the water, earth, tree and fire, in fact the whole creation. Thus revived, the Evil Spirit in gratitude granted her wish that men should desire her. Then, with all the demons, Ahriman rose to attack the world. He broke through the sky which was as afraid of him 'as a sheelp of a wolf'. Passing through the waters he entered the middle of the earth and assaulted the material creation. The earth became so dark that at noon it seemed like a dark night. Horrible creatures were released over the face of the earth and their pollution spread so thickly that not even as much as the point of a needle was free from their contamination. The tree was poisoned and died. Turning to the ox and Gayomart, Ahriman afflicted them with 'Greed, Needfulness, Disease, Hunger, Illness, Vice and Lethargy'. Before the Evil Spirit came to the ox Ohrmazd gave her cannabis to ease her discomfort in the throes of death, but at last her milk dried up and she died. Man, the chief ally of God and the arch-opponent of evil, was then set upon by the might of a thousand 'death-producing' demons, but even they could not kill him until his appointed time was come, for man's rule had been fixed for a period of thirty years. Everything was being destroyed, smoke and darkness were mingled with the fire, and the whole creation was disfigured. For ninety days the spiritual beings contested with the demons in the material world. Every archangel had an opposing arch-demon, every good thing was attacked by its counterpart: Falsehood against Truth, the Spell of Sorcery against the Holy Word, Excess and Deficiency against Temperance, Idleness against Diligence, Darkness against Light, Unforgiveness against Mercy. Throughout the whole material existence and the firmament, everything was attacked and finally even man was killed.

The assault of Ahriman now seemed to be completely successful and the Good Creation to be totally ruined or destroyed. Disorderly motion, the production of evil, appeared to have won a victory over order and peace; and the work of the Wise Lord was an apparent failure.

A festive meal among Irani Zoroastrians.

Yet despite all appearances this was not the end of Good, for troubles were just beginning for Evil. Ahriman, after his apparent victory, sought to return to his natural home of darkness, but found his way blocked by both the Spirit of the Sky, clad in armour like a warrior, and the *fravashis* of men. The *fravashis* are a famed group in Persian mythology. As the whole of the material creation has a spiritual origin, man has a heavenly self, his fravashi. Whatever evil man may do on earth his genuine heavenly self is unaffected, and it is only the earthly man, not the fravashi, which will suffer for his sins in hell (although one text does state that even the fravashis can go to hell). The host of just fravashis elected of their own free will to assist Ohrmazd in his battle and stood arrayed as 'valiant cavaliers with spears in hand', preventing Ahriman from escaping from the prison into which he had burst.

Thus imprisoned in a hostile world Ahriman discovered that life was beginning to flourish again. The rains were produced by Sirius; the waters washed the vile creatures into the holes in the ground, and the earth became productive. Nor was this all, for in Ahriman's apparent victory lay the seeds of his own defeat. As the ox died, fifty-five species of corn and twelve species of medicinal herbs grew from its limbs and its seed passed to the moon where it was purified, giving rise to the different species of animals. So, too, man as he died passed seed into the earth. Thus from his body, made of metal, the earth received the different kinds of metal, and from his sperm grew the first human couple, Mashye and Mashyane.

Just as the sky, the waters (Sirius), the ox and man thus waged battle with the Destructive Spirit so, too, did the plants, the earth, the fire and other components of the creation. Life was triumphant. Death, the work of the Evil Spirit, stood defeated, for out of death came life, and life more abundant than before. From the one ox came the different species of animals, and from man came the parents of the human race.

Never from the time of creation until the rehabilitation in purity has this earth been devoid of men, nor will it ever be, and the Destructive Spirit, not being good, cannot understand this will to succeed.
D.i.D. 34:2, ZDT, p. 261

A manuscript of the Zoroastrian bible, the Avesta, *with an interlinear translation into Middle Persian or Pahlavi. This page tells part of the story of the primordial twins.*

Though Ahriman may kill individuals, mankind as a whole ever increases, not only rendering his assaults failures, but even making them work against him.

Man's First Parents

The first human couple grew from the seed of Gayomart which had passed into the earth. At first they grew together in the shape of a plant in such a manner that man and woman were indistinguishable. Together they formed the tree whose fruit was the ten races of mankind. When they finally assumed human form the Wise Lord instructed them in their responsibilities:

You are the seed of man, you are the parents of the world, you have been given by me as the best perfect devotion; think good thoughts, speak good words, do good deeds, and do not worship the demons.
G.Bd. 14:11, BTA. p. 129

But evil lurked at hand to seduce them away from their true path. Ahriman attacked their thoughts and they uttered the first falsehood–they declared the Evil Spirit to be the creator. Attributing the origin of the world to evil was thus man's first sin; for the Zoroastrian it is the gravest sin.

From this moment on the first couple began to wander from the life God had planned for them; their orientation in life was lost. They offered a sacrifice which was not pleasing to the gods, they began to drink milk and although they shared in work–a great Zoroastrian virtue–by digging wells, smelting iron and making wooden tools, the result was not the peace, progress and harmony which should characterise the world but violence and malice. The demons corrupted them spiritually by inducing them to worship them rather than God, and morally by taking away their desire for intercourse for fifty years. Already in this myth we can see some of the distinctive Zoroastrian teachings emerging–the outlook on the world, on work and now on procreation. Celibacy is no virtue in Zoroastrianism; it is, indeed, the very opposite, for it fails to increase the Good Creation of the Wise Lord, thereby neglecting a fundamental religious duty of all men and women. Even when the first couple did produce offspring they devoured them until the Wise Lord took away the sweetness of children. Then, at last, Mashye and Mashyane fulfilled their function by giving birth to the whole human race.

God and Man

The world existed for six thousand years before the assault of Ahriman. For three thousand years it existed in purely spiritual form; for another three thousand it took material form, but was still combined with the spiritual. The world was created by Ohrmazd to do battle with evil. Ahriman's attack on the world produced in it all moral and physical evil. The world, plants, animals, men, even the cosmos, shook at his attack, but try as he might Ahriman could not overcome the principle of life. As the first man died he emitted seed which gave rise to the first human couple. Although they in turn were submitted to all manner of onslaughts and temptations, mankind continued to increase.

The basic conviction is that the history of the world is the history of the conflict between good and evil. In this conflict man is essentially the helper of God. He is not created for sport as in some Hindu traditions, nor as a being to whom God can manifest his glory. God needs man as man needs God. The world in which man lives, although it is defiled by the attacks of evil, is basically good, for God is its father and mother. To deny this is one of the basic Zoroastrian sins. Unlike the Hellenistic religions, the Zoroastrians did not compare matter unfavourably with spirit; they held that both should be in perfect harmony for the ideal existence, an existence to which history moves with the end of the world, or better, the renovation of the world.

Myths of the End

Eschatology, the doctrine of the last things, is a central and famous element of the Zoroastrian teaching. It is thought by many that this doctrine was a source

کوشتو سروت

کنشن ایرپرستان

روشن فه مینشن کو آن ایرپران روشن او تاریک

کام

آن زن مرد که

نن کو مان فراورن از آن

آوارون فراورن کنشن

سا

کو که آن کار فه نن

پیش آموختش آن پادداهشن

کو مان فراورن آموختن پادداهشن

of influence for both Eastern and Western beliefs–Hinduism and Buddhism in the East and Judaism and Christianity in the West.

Within Zoroastrianism there are two parts to the doctrine of the end, the end of the individual at death and the 'end' of the world. We shall look at each in turn.

Whereas belief in a life after death became a part of Jewish theology at a relatively late date, it has been a dominant part of Persian thought from earliest times. Eternity is not just a promise of a future reward, it is in fact man's true home, for that which appears to destroy man–death–is the weapon of the Evil Spirit. Man was made for life and not for death. If death were the last word then the Evil Spirit, not God, would be the ultimate victor.

Life after death

After death the soul hovers round the body for three nights. The first night it contemplates the words of its past life, the second the thoughts, and the third the deeds. These three nights are a time of regret for the soul, regret at the death of the body, and a time of yearning for the reunification of the body with the soul. During this time the demons lurk close at hand, ever eager to inflict suffering and punishment regardless of whether it is justified. The soul, therefore, needs the protection of the just Sraosha, protection effected by the offerings and prayers of the relatives of the deceased. The three nights are also a time of anguish and consolation–anguish at the thought of the soul's misdeeds in life, consolation at the thought of its merits.

At dawn after the third night each soul proceeds to its judgment. During the life of the individual a store of merits or faults has been laid up in the House of Song. These are weighed in the balances before the eyes of the judges, Mithra, Sraosha and Rashnu. No favour is shown on any side, either for the rich or for the poor, for the weak or for the strong. Every man is judged entirely on his own life. If the good thoughts, words and deeds outweigh the evil, the soul passes to heaven; if the evil outweigh the good, then the soul is sent to hell but if the two are exactly equal the soul proceeds to an intermediate place, Hamestagan. The Zoroastrians cannot accept the Christian idea that the life, death and sacrifice of one can atone for the sins of the many–such an outcome of the judgment would be unbecoming to the justice of a man, much less the justice of God.

As the souls leave the place of judgment they are met by a guide. The righteous are met by a fragrant wind and a maiden more beautiful than man has ever met before. Astounded at her beauty the soul asks who she is and whence she came. She replies, 'I am the Conscience of thine own self'. She is the manifestation of the soul's own thoughts, words and deeds. The wicked soul, on the other hand, is met by a foul stench and a naked, most loathesomely diseased old hag, the manifestation of its thoughts, words and deeds.

The soul then proceeds to the Chinvat bridge. This bridge has two faces which it may present: to the righteous it is broad and easy to cross, to the wicked it turns and presents a sharp edge like that of a sword so that when the soul is half way across it falls into the abyss of hell. As the righteous soul passes over the bridge it sees the spiritual Yazatas, the victorious Fire dispels the darkness, and spiritually purified, the soul is conducted to heaven. The wicked soul suffers great agonies; it cries and laments like a wolf trapped in a pit, but no help is forthcoming. It is compelled against its will to cross over the bridge by its evil actions, which assume the form of a wild beast that terrifies it and makes it step forward on to the bridge. Taking three steps, the steps of evil thoughts, evil words and evil deeds, it falls headlong into hell and suffers all manner of afflictions.

One barrier which wicked and righteous alike are said to face is the river of tears made by the mourners. Excessive lamentation and weeping swell the river, making it more difficult for the soul to pass over. Zoroastrians consider excessive lamentation a sin because it injures the health of the mourner yet it is of no help to the deceased. What is much more useful is the performance of the correct rituals, for they can be of great comfort to the soul.

The souls of the dead crossing the bridge of judgment, the Chinvat bridge, from which the wicked fall into hell.

The After Life

We turn now to the fate of the soul after it has crossed over or fallen from the Chinvat bridge. But before the Zoroastrian concepts of heaven and hell are described a word needs to be said about the general picture of the after life. When the soul passes on to the place of reward or punishment it does not enter an eternal state. The idea of eternal punishment in hell is morally repugnant to a Zoroastrian, who believes that the only purpose of any just punishment is to reform or correct. A parent who punished his or her child simply for the sake of punishment would be classed as cruel. How, then, can one attribute such an action to God? Eternal suffering in hell cannot be corrective, a good god could not, therefore, allow it. Thus the Zoroastrian hell is a temporary existence where the punishment, though very severe, is a corrective one made to fit the crime, so that when good ultimately triumphs all men will be resurrected, both from heaven and hell, and the whole creation will be united with its source, the wholly good God.

Heaven

The description of heaven is contained in the writings of the righteous Viraf, who is said to have been transported in a vision to heaven and hell so that he might tell the faithful what lay before them. Led over the Chinvat bridge by Sraosha and other heavenly beings, he was met on the other side by the heavenly fravashis who conducted him to Hamestagen, the abode of those whose good and evil deeds are equal. Their punishment is simply from heat and cold, no more. From there he passed to the various stations of the heavens.

First Viraf went to the star station 'where good thoughts are received with hospitality'. There the souls, whose radiance glitters like the stars, sit on thrones, splendid and full of glory. At the next station, the moon station, are those with whom 'good words find hospitality'. Although these souls may not have performed all the requirements of the Zoroastrian faith they are given their place in heaven because they have performed many good works and now 'Their brightness is like unto the brightness of the moon'. The third station is that of the sun where good rulers are rewarded for their faithful administration of their heavy task. The fourth station is that of Garodman where Viraf was greeted by Vohu Manah, Good Mind, and led into the presence of Ahura Mazda. There Viraf was shown the different dwellings of the righteous, those who were liberal, those who were faithful in the performance of the Zoroastrian ritual and those women who had been good and faithful wives, considering their husbands as lords. Viraf was also shown the dwelling place of the agriculturalists and artisans, of those who had carried out their work faithfully, together with the places of the shepherds, the heads of villages, teachers, enquirers (into the Good Religion) and peace-seekers. All dwell among fine carpets and cushions in great pleasure and joy.

Hell

Viraf, after returning to the bridge, was then taken to hell that he might see the lot of the wicked. In the first three nights after death they suffer as much distress as a man experiences in the whole of a hard life in the world. Led by the old hag who personifies the consciences of the wicked, Viraf passed through the places of evil thought, evil words and evil deeds into hell. There he experienced intense cold and heat, darkness so intense that it could be grasped and a stench so powerful that it could be cut with a knife. He saw the 'greedy jaws of hell, like the most frightful pit'. Everyone in hell is packed in so tight that life is intolerable, yet all believe that they are alone and time drags so slowly that after three days they believe that the nine thousand-year period of the world has elapsed. Everywhere there are vile creatures seemingly as high as mountains, which tear and seize the souls of the wicked. The miserable wretches suffer from the extremes of driving snow and the heat of the brisk-burning fire, from foul stench, stones and ashes.

Each soul is subjected to severe, but appropriate, punishment for its misdeeds.

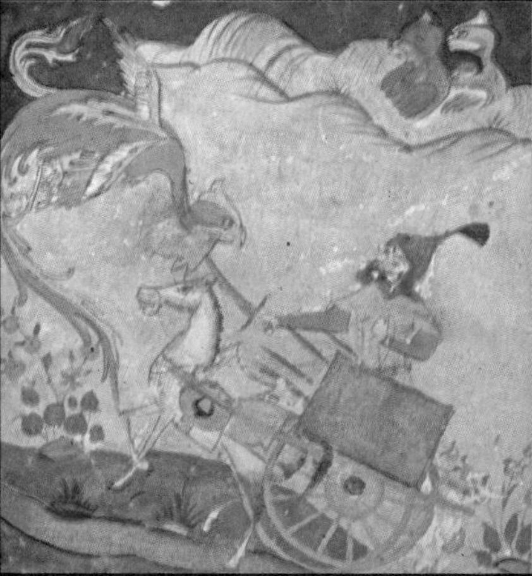

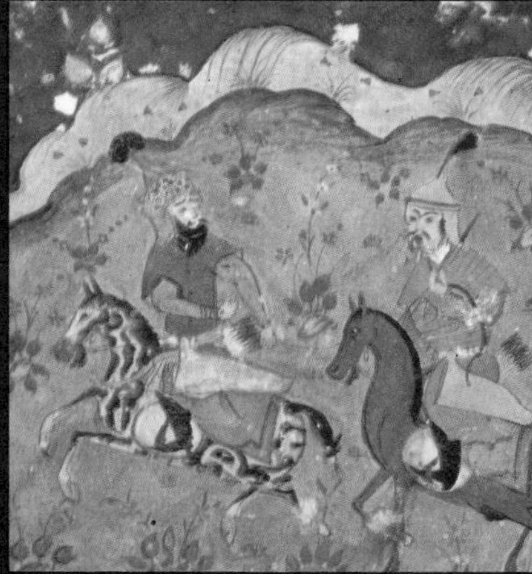

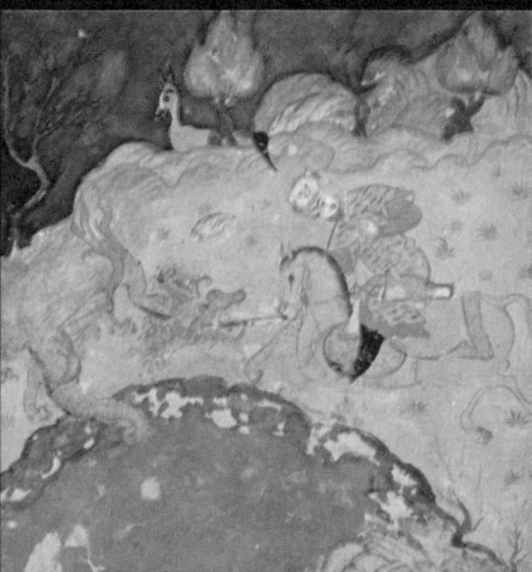

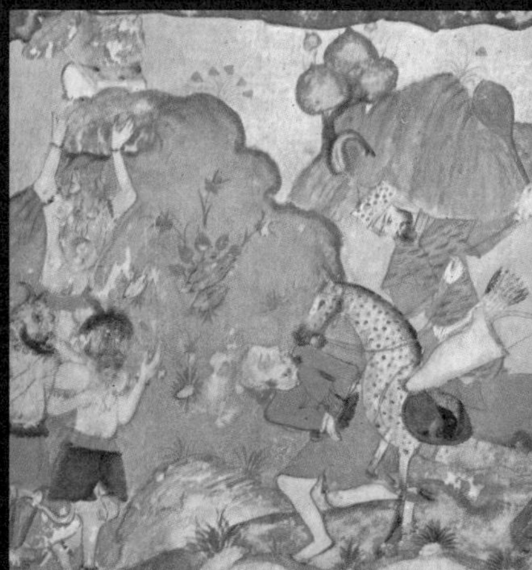

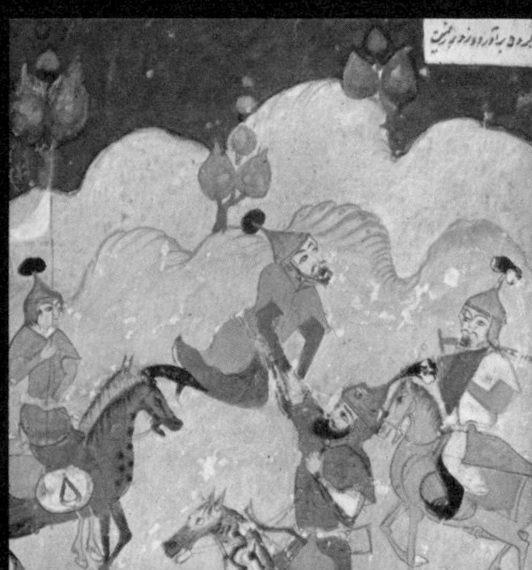

Rustam is a legendary hero of Persian tradition. He was not born in the normal way but as a result of the incantations of a wizard at the behest of the mythological Simurgh bird with the aid of its magical feathers. A lion of a man, as tall as eight men, he rode a horse of magnificent prowess. After searching the country he caught one set aside for him from birth; it had the strength of an elephant and the speed of a racing camel. Famed for his strength, Rustam saved his monarchs from prison. He slew dragons, demons and great warriors in battle, himself enduring treachery, attack, even capture by demons. On one occasion he was dropped into the ocean among monsters but escaped and finally triumphed. The author is indebted to Professor Sir Harold Bailey for permission to reproduce these illustrations from an unpublished seventeenth-century manuscript of the Shah name *from Bukhara.*

The mythological bird Simurgh and the ambitious prince Isfandiyar, who was defeated by Rustam with Simurgh's help.

Rakhsh, Rustam's mighty steed, is lassoed and caught by the hero.

Rustam defeating a dragon in order to save his monarch, king Kavus.

Rustam, led by the captive Awlad to the demons' abode, overpowers the Great White Demon in order to save King Kavus.

The proud Turanian warrior Puladvand is defeated by Rustam.

Rustam saving the warrior Bizhan from a pit in which he was cast by Afrasiyab, the ruler of Turan.

To capture Rustam the demon Akwan took away the ground on which the hero slept and then threw him into the ocean.

A woman who had committed adultery was suspended by the breasts to hell; and noxious creatures seized her whole body.
AV. 24, Haug, p. 171

A man who had given false measure in trading they ever forced to measure dust and ashes, and they ever gave him to eat.
AV. 27, Haug, p. 172

A ruler who was unmerciful was held in the atmosphere, and fifty demons ever flogged before and behind, with darting serpents.
AV. 28, Haug, p. 173

A man who had ever been selfish with many riches remained stretched on a rack, and a thousand demons trampled upon him with great brutality and violence.
AV. 31, p. 174

The individual punishments are ameliorated according to the good deeds performed. Thus a man who had committed adultery was set in a boiling cauldron, but because he had killed many vile creatures with his foot this was left outside the cauldron and did not suffer like the rest of his body.

These texts are interesting not only for their general picture of heaven and hell as a place of stern but corrective punishment, but also for the details given of what a Zoroastrian considers to be a religious sin: giving false measure, unjust rule by a monarch, a woman having an abortion, homosexuality, meanness and so on.

Both heaven and hell are here described in material terms. Heaven is above the earth and hell under the earth. The delights and torments are also described in physical terms. Yet the texts stress that the delights and sufferings far exceed anything which is experienced on earth, and in view of the stress on the *soul's* experiences it may be that this post-mortem fate was thought of as a spiritual experience, even though there was no language to express it as such.

One further point should be noted, the idea of the ascent of the soul through various heavens. This is usually thought to be a trace of a very ancient concept which reappears in a number of guises in different traditions. It is possible, for example, that the ascent of the soul may be depicted on the reliefs at Commagene where the king is shown shaking hands with various gods. Such an idea does occur in Gnosticism and perhaps in Mithraism where the initiate passes through a number of different grades on the spiritual 'ladder'.

The Universal Judgment

As we have seen, the Zoroastrians believe that the history of the world lasts for twelve thousand years. The final period in which evil is defeated is thought to have started with the birth of Zoroaster, so that in Zoroastrian belief we are living in the final period of world history.

The final period of history is itself divided into four lesser periods, each being symbolised by a metal: gold for the period when the Good Religion was revealed to Zoroaster, silver for the period when his royal patron accepted the religion, steel for the Sasanian period and iron for this present age when the religion is declining. Although it is in this period that evil is defeated the battle is not one long success story for the forces of good, but a series of pendulum swings when first good and then evil appears to be triumphant. During this final world age of three thousand years the Zoroastrians expect three saviours to come, at one-thousand-year intervals. The first was expected a thousand years after Zoroaster. Since Zoroaster is generally thought to have lived about 600 BC this means that the first two saviours should have made their appearance by now. How Zoroastrians overcome this problem we shall see later. They believe that the period of iron, the period of the decline of the religion before the appearance of the first saviour, still continues.

The Kushana Mozdoano, probably derived from Mazda Vano, 'Mazda the triumphant'. It is interesting that the supreme god is here represented on horseback. This is unlike the Achaemenid symbolism but resembles the equestrian imagery used by the Sasanians. Although this type is rare it does bring out the triumphant warrior character of God.

The Period of Iron

This period is marked by what the Judeo-Christian tradition calls the 'signs of the end'–manifestations of the horror and power of evil. Demons of the race of Aeshma (Fury) with their 'dishevelled hair' will attack Persia. The result will be the complete destruction of ordered life in the land. Family and social life will disintegrate, and the respect for truth, love and the Good Religion will decline. The disruption will be cosmic also: the sun and moon will not give their proper light, there will be darkness and gloom on earth, earthquakes, droughts and famine. There will be battles on earth and life appears to be so horrible that Zoroaster, to whom all this is said to be revealed in a vision, prays that he may not live at that time. This onslaught of evil is parallel to that at the beginning of world history. Then the Evil Spirit afflicted the sun, shook the earth so that mountains appeared and inflicted disorder on order. Similarly at the end, the sun's light will be affected, earthquakes will break out and family, social and religious life will be rendered chaotic.

At last a shower of stars will appear in the sky, marking the birth of a righteous prince who will overcome the evil armies and restore the Persian lands and the throne of the Good Religion prior to the birth of the first saviour.

The First Saviour

The saviour, Aushedar, 'the developer of righteousness', though he is to be born of a virgin, will also be the offspring of the great prophet, Zoroaster. The myth relates that Zoroaster's seed has been preserved in a lake. At the approach of the millennium his seed will impregnate a fifteen-year-old virgin while she is bathing and the saviour will be conceived.

When he reaches the age of thirty the sun will stand still for ten days at the noon-day position, Rapithwin, where it had stood before the first attack of Ahriman. The saviour will confer with the archangels, and he will bring with him the revelation first brought by Zoroaster. Through his coming something of the paradisal state returns. For three years men will live more harmoniously and part of the evil creation, the wolf species, will disappear. Thus the coming of the first saviour gives the first foretaste of the perfection to come, the combination of primeval order with the Good Religion brought by Zoroaster. The renovation of the universe is not, however, complete. Evil still exists and will assert itself once more.

The texts do not agree over the nature of the outbreak of evil which will occur at the end of this millennium. Some state that the enemies of Persia will return and suppress the Good Religion and the state, but this appears to be a historicising of the mythical belief contained in other texts where the outbreak of evil takes the form of a terrible winter produced through the sorcery of the demon Malkus. The snow and hail will destroy a large part of mankind. Yet before the coming of the second saviour good will again triumph for the earth will be re-peopled from the vara built by Yima (see p. 40). In this re-populated earth disease will no longer prove fatal and death will come about only through old age or murder. Thus Ahriman's greatest weapon, death, will begin to lose its power prior to the birth of the second saviour.

The Second Saviour

Like his predecessor, the second saviour, Aushedar-mah, will be born of a virgin who has been impregnated by the seed of Zoroaster preserved in a lake. Whereas the sun stood still for ten days at the coming of Aushedar it will now stand at the noonday position for twenty days and the creation will flourish for six instead of three years. During the millennium of Aushedar wolves had disappeared from the face of the earth and now more members of the evil creation will disappear, snakes for instance. The original paradisal state will draw yet nearer. Men will no longer need to eat meat, they will become vegetarians and drink only water.

But despite this growing power of the Good Creation and the gradual expulsion of evil, the powers of darkness are far from finished. Evil will re-assert itself in the form of Azhi Dahaka, the monster who had been imprisoned in a cave in Mount Demavend by Thraetaona (see p. 43). He will escape and rushing into the world will perpetrate sin, devouring one-third of mankind and the animal world. He will smite the sacred elements of the fire, water and vegetation. But another ancient hero, Keresaspa, will be resurrected and will finally rid the world of this evil being.

The millennium of each saviour thus follows a neat pattern: prior to the saviour's birth good will be in the ascendant, the miraculous appearance of the saviour will bring creation nearer to the paradisal state and the powers of evil will be reduced. Yet evil will, on each occasion, launch an assault which threatens to destroy mankind until it is overcome through the work of one of the primeval heroes.

The Third and Final Saviour

Soshyant, the final saviour, will be conceived by a virgin in the same way as his predecessors, but with his coming the complete and final triumph of good will arrive. All disease, death and persecution will be overcome, vegetation will flourish perpetually and mankind will eat only spiritual food. The world is now to be perfectly and finally renovated. The dead will be raised by Soshyant from the spot where life had departed from them. All men will then proceed to the last judgment where everyone will see his good and evil deeds. There the righteous will appear as conspicuous among the wicked as white sheep are among black. After this judgment the wicked will return to hell and the righteous to heaven for a period of three days and three nights to receive their due reward. Whereas the bridge-judgment, with its ensuing reward or punishment, was concerned with the soul, the last judgment, following the resurrection, will be concerned with the whole man, body and soul, so that finally man may praise the creator in his total being, in the perfect harmony of spirit and matter. First, however, all men will have to pass through a stream of molten metal. The stream of metal which has already levelled the earth to its primeval state of a plain will sweep over all men that they, too, may be made uniform in purity. The gift of immortality will be conferred when Soshyant, acting as priest, celebrates the final sacrifice with the last animal to die in the service of man, the ox whose role in primeval history we have already noted. From the fat of that ox and the mythical White Hom from the cosmic ocean the elixir of immortality will be prepared.

The texts then relate the final defeat of evil, although this may not have been the chronological position the event held in Zoroastrian belief. Each of the heavenly beings will seize and destroy his demonic opponent until the only survivors, Ahriman and Az, flee back to hell. The molten metal which has levelled the earth and swept over men will flow into hell, consuming the stench and contamination which characterises that place, so that all evil will be rendered impotent if not annihilated. Unfortunately the texts are not clear on Ahriman's precise fate. The hole which the Evil Spirit had made on his entry into the world will be sealed up. With the earth levelled and man restored to his ideal unity of body and soul the whole creation will be once more the perfect combination of spirit and matter that God intended it to be.

It is wrong to call this event the end of the world, for in Zoroastrianism it is not that. The end of the world would be the victory of Ahriman. It is rather, as the Zoroastrians themselves call it, the Renovation. The world is restored to the perfect state it enjoyed before the assault of Ahriman. But it is even more than that. Matters have not simply returned to their former state, for now Ahriman is no more and Ohrmazd reigns, not only all good, all knowing, but now all powerful also.

Mount Demavend, the mythological prison in which the demon Azhi Dahaka is bound until the end of history. It is easy to see how myths developed around this noble and mysterious mountain, which towers up to 18,000 feet above sea level.

The figure on this Luristan bronze has been identified as Zurvan giving birth to twins, Ohrmazd and Ahriman, surrounded by the three ages of man: youth (bottom left) maturity (left) and old age (right). The figures are said to be holding the sacred barsom twigs. This may be an anachronistic interpretation. Perhaps the myth underlying the scene developed into the Zurvanite myth.

ZURVANISM, A ZOROASTRIAN HERESY

So far in this book attention has been focused on the orthodox teaching and mythology of Zoroastrianism. Even the ancient beliefs that have been expounded are preserved only in Zoroastrian texts and they themselves have been incorporated into the Zoroastrian system. But, as with any religion, different beliefs and mythologies grew in Zoroastrianism, the main dissident group being the Zurvanites.

Although some scholars believe Zurvanism to be a pre-Zoroastrian tradition it is usually thought that it developed during the Achaemenid period as a result of Babylonian influence. It may have been very popular during the Parthian period but it was during the Sasanian period that it appears to have come to the forefront. Even during the Sasanian period, however, it probably flourished as an intellectual movement within the Zoroastrian Church, rather than as a distinct sect. Zurvanite mythology is very difficult to reconstruct as we have no purely Zurvanite text, only the accounts of outside observers and the occasional polemic of Zoroastrians. Such evidence must obviously be used with caution.

The name of the 'sect' is derived from their name for the ultimate being, Zurvan, Time. Zurvan, they believed, was the ultimate source of both good and evil, the Father of the brothers Ohrmazd and Ahriman. In Zurvanite belief the Absolute contained within his being the polarity of good and evil. The Zurvanites sought a unity behind the dualism of orthodox Zoroastrianism. The implications they drew from this belief were enormous, but before discussing these we shall set out the myth as it is preserved in the reports of foreigners, principally Eznik, an Armenian.

Before the existence of earth or heaven the great and ultimate being Zurvan existed alone. Wanting a son he offered sacrifice for a thousand years. The offering of sacrifice does not imply that he was praying to any other being, for in Persian belief the offering of sacrifice has merit or power in and of itself. After a thousand years, however, he began to doubt the fulfilment of his desire. He doubted the power of sacrifice to produce a son, Ohrmazd, who would create the heavens and the earth. At the moment of his doubt twins were conceived within himself, for Zurvan, being the undifferentiated one, was androgynous. The twins were Ohrmazd, the fulfilment of his desire, and

Ahriman, the personification of his doubt. Zurvan vowed that he would give the gift of kingship to whichever son emerged from the womb first. Ohrmazd, already displaying his great characteristic of omniscience, was aware of this and informed his brother, whereupon Ahriman ripped open the womb, presented himself to his father, declaring 'I am your son Ohrmazd'.

And Zurvan said: 'My son is light and fragrant, but thou art dark and stinking.' And he wept most bitterly.
ZDT. p. 208

When Ohrmazd appeared Zurvan recognised him immediately as the fulfilment of his desire and offered him the symbol of priesthood, the barsom twigs. In order that he should not break his vow of the gift of kingship for the first born, he gave Ahriman the rule of the world for a period of nine thousand years. To Ohrmazd he granted rule above so that Ohrmazd created the heavens and the earth.

Ahriman, meanwhile, as in orthodox Zoroastrianism, created the demons, poverty and all that is evil and perverse. Ohrmazd represents all that is good in Zurvan, Ahriman all that is evil. Behind the manifold experiences and features of life the Zurvanites saw one ultimate source which encompassed all within the one being, the polarity of light and dark, good and evil. Evil exists in the world not as a result of error, nor ultimately as the miscreation of the Evil Spirit, but as a potentiality within the nature of the Absolute. The purpose of the battle between good and evil is to restore the unity within the Absolute which was shattered by divine doubt.

The implications drawn from this myth were mainly of a philosophical nature and because of this it has been plausibly argued that Zurvanism was mainly the religion of the intelligentsia. There appears to have been more than one form of Zurvanism, but whether these differences ever gave rise to distinct sects of Zurvanism is rather unlikely.

One of the developments of the belief in Zurvan was the idea of a materialistic evolution of the universe, a development which may have taken place under foreign influence. The idea was that the creation of the universe was not an act of God but an evolutionary development of formless primeval matter, Infinite Time and Space (Zurvan) into all that has form, the finite. The Infinite thus becomes the finite. This process can, of course, stand without belief in a creator and it seems that with this 'evolutionary' idea went a denial of heaven, hell and all future rewards or punishments. In short, this attribution of the evolution of the world from the primal Time/Space, Zurvan, was based on a thoroughly materialistic interpretation of the universe, fundamentally alien to the orthodox Zoroastrian belief in a creator, a life after death and a stress on rewards or punishments.

The evolution of the world from Time was taken by some to imply that the world was bounded and controlled by the heavenly sphere. In terms of astrological myth this meant that the fate of the individual was pre-determined by the cosmic battle between the twelve signs of the Zodiac, representing the forces of good, and the seven planets which oppress creation by ruling over its fate. This fatalism, foreign to orthodox Zoroastrianism, exerted quite a degree of influence in Persian thought. It not only entered some Zoroastrian writings, but also appears in some passages of the vast epic, the *Shah name*. The poet recounts the questioning of one Zal by the Magian hierarchy. As a test of his religious knowledge he has to interpret a set of riddles. One such is about a man who

with a great sharp scythe strides insolently towards the meadow (full of greenery and streams). Moist and dry he mows down, and if thou make supplication he will not hear thee.

The interpretation of this riddle is that the man with the scythe is Time, and we are the grass. All are treated alike by the mower, no account is taken of

youth or old age, all in his path are cut down. The nature of the world is such that if it were not for death in the world there would be no birth either:

We enter in at one door and pass out of another: Time counts our every breath. *ZDT. pp. 240f*

This gloomy outlook on life, the cynical attitude to birth and death are far removed from the optimistic, positive attitude of orthodox Zoroastrians.

A cynical attitude to women is thought by many to have been another feature of Zurvanism. In some reconstructions of the Zurvanite 'fall narratives' the evil Jahi, the whore, first united herself with Ahriman and then seduced the righteous man, Gayomart. If this was so then the Zurvanites believed that it was woman's sexual desire which was the cause of evil in the world. According to one Zoroastrian text, the *Bundahishn,* Ohrmazd admits that although women are helpful to him because they give birth to men he would never have created women if he could have found any other vessel. But search as he did in the waters and the earth, among plants and cattle, in the mountains and valleys, he could find no alternative. This is often taken as an example of Zurvanite influence on Zoroastrianism. It may also be, of course, that there were misogynists and 'oddities' among traditional Zoroastrians and that this was not a specifically Zurvanite belief. Such phenomena exist in most religions–Christianity has never been lacking in this respect despite the importance of Mary–so the same may apply to Zoroastrianism. There is a great danger in labelling every unusual Zoroastrian belief 'Zurvanite'.

The main differences between Zurvanism and Zoroastrianism, then, are those based on the idea of the Absolute as Infinite Space/Time; the nature of Zurvan, the belief in Ohrmazd and Ahriman as twins, the idea that Ahriman ruled the world for nine thousand years, fatalism and materialism.

This Luristan bronze is thought by some to portray Zurvan, flanked by the two spirits, Ohrmazd and Ahriman. However, it is by no means certain whether the Zurvanite myth dates back to this early period.

A miniature showing an astrologer with his instruments. Astrology played an important part in Zurvanite belief.

The birth of Mithras from the cosmic egg. The god holds the flaming torch as the light entering the world and the dagger with which he will slay the bull. He is surrounded by the signs of the zodiac as a sign of the cosmic significance of his birth. The egg birth is due to Orphic influence.

THE MYTHOLOGY OF MITHRAISM

Mithra is an important god in the history of many different countries at many different times; his worship spread as far west as the north of England and as far east as India. First worshipped thousands of years ago, he is still venerated by Zoroastrians today.

In ancient India where his name appears as Mitra, Friendship or Contract, he was usually invoked with another god, Varuna, True Speech, in the formula Mitra-Varuna. The two are often described in human terms. Together they mount their shining chariot, which has the trappings of any earthly chariot. They dwell in a golden mansion wich has a thousand pillars and a thousand doors. But despite this imagery there are no stories or myths told about them. The imagery is used simply to draw out the character of these two figures.

Mitra and Varuna are described as cosmic rulers upholding order in the world of gods and men, for Contract and True Speech are the basis of all ordered life in the cosmos, in religion and in society. Through the observance of the Contract mankind is united and falsehood overcome, and by faithful fulfilment of one's ritual duties the sun is made to shine and the rains to fall.

From Persia we have a hymn to Mithra which is usually dated about 450 BC in its present form, although the material it uses is much older than this. As in India Mithra has a great palace, one built by the creator in which there is

no night or darkness, no wind cold or hot, no deadly illness, no defilement produced by evil gods.
Yt. 10:49–50 AHM p. 99

Mithra rides forth in his chariot pulled by four white immortal horses shod in gold and silver. He is

the first supernatural god to approach across the Harā, in front of the immortal swift-horsed sun . . . the first to seize the beautiful gold-painted mountain tops, from there the most mighty surveys the whole land inhabited by Iranians.
Yt. 10, 12–13, AHM p. 79

In Persia, as in India, the mythical imagery is used only to bring out the character of the god Contract. Mithra is the one who preserved Order or

The famous lion-headed figure of Mithraism which some have identified as Zurvan, the high god, and others as Ahriman, the devil. What few scholars point out is that this statue has been heavily restored. In the photograph at the side can be seen the statue in its original state.

Truth. He it is who attacks and defeats the demons of the Lie, he it is who judges when the contract concerning the different periods of world history is completed. In his concern for Truth he judges the soul at death and brandishes his mace over hell three times each day so that the demons do not inflict greater punishment on sinners than they deserve. One scholar who lived among Zoroastrians for some time tells how a Parsi mother in Karachi, finding one of her grandchildren fibbing, admonished him to remember that Mithra was watching and would know the truth.

The hymn to Mithra expresses this idea of the god Contract preserving Truth and Order in the picture imagery of a 'mighty strong warrior' with a pike of silver, gold armour and strong shoulders smashing the heads of evil gods and men, before whom

the Fiendish Spirit . . . malignant Wrath . . . long-handed Procrastination . . . all supernatural evil gods . . . recoil in fear.
st. 97 AHM p. 121

To the Persians Persia was naturally the land of the Contract and we find that before going into battle against 'anti-Mithraean countries' the soldiers prayed to Mithra 'at the manes of their horses' and a Roman historian records that before going into battle the Persian King

with his generals and staff passed around the ranks of the armed men, praying to the sun and Mithra and the sacred eternal fire.
Quintius Rufus, History of Alexander, IV, 13, 2

In modern Zoroastrianism Mithra plays a very important part in the ritual. All priests are initiated in the 'portico of Mithra', the *dar i Mithr*, and on initiation they are invested with the mace of Mithra as a symbol of their duty to fight against the powers of evil. All the most sacred rituals are offered under his protection and one of the great Zoroastrian festivals is the Mihragan, a festival in honour of 'Mithra, Judge of Iran', a festival still celebrated in Persia for five days with great rejoicing and in a spirit of deep devotion.

Some scholars believe that the great warrior and judge played a more important role in the final judgment and battle against evil than the texts at first sight might suggest. A number of Persian texts hint that this is so, but it is difficult to be certain about it. One interesting possibility has come to light. In the early Christian world there circulated two supposedly Persian prophecies or oracles about a saviour to come. In neither case is the saviour named, but in both cases it is possible that Mithra is the figure behind the imagery. One prophecy speaks of a star that will lead Magi to the birthplace of the saviour in a cave on a mountain top, a prophecy that would make an interesting background to the gospel story of the magi if it could be identified and dated with certainty. The other Oracle foretells the appearance of a saviour at the end of the world who will come with fire to destroy the wicked and save the righteous. If these are Mithraic then we have a new and very interesting dimension to the god's character.

So far we have looked at Mithra in the Indian and Persian setting. He was also, of course, an important Roman god (Mithras). Just how this ironic twist of history transferred one of the most revered Persian gods to being one of the most popular gods of her arch-enemy, Rome, is something which scholars would dearly like to know. Presumably his worship spread westwards through the Persian satellites in Asia Minor, Armenia, Cappadocia, Cilicia and Pontus. Just how and when is the problem. One possibility is the visit of Tiridates, king of Armenia, who went to Rome in AD 66 to receive his crown from Nero. Addressing the emperor he said:

I am come to thee as my god, to worship thee as I worship Mithra, and I will be as thou shalt determine. For thou art my Destiny and my Fate.
Dio Cassius 63:10

A Sasanian dish showing king Peroz (AD 459–484) hunting. The style employed on this and several other dishes is very similar to that used in the scene of Mithra hunting in the Roman temple at Dura Europos—notice in particular the position of the horse (the flying gallop), the frontal position of the rider and the style of the leading boar. The Romans either employed a Persian artist or knew of the Persian style.

right *A scene showing Mithras hunting, from Dura Europos. Although it comes from the Roman cult, the style of the clothes, the position of the figure and horse and the pattern of the animals are completely Persian. The scene has been interpreted by some as symbolic of the god hunting the forces of evil.*

Tiridates is also said to have initiated Nero into 'the banquets of the magi', possibly a reference to the Mithraic communion meal. It may be that the visit of the Armenian king to Rome, with his enormous train of followers, brought in its wake the worship of Mithra. Perhaps the most likely explanation of this 'transfer' of the god is the recruitment of Mithra-worshipping auxiliaries from Asia Minor into the Roman legions, who were then moved throughout the Roman Empire. But whenever and however Mithra entered Rome, by the time of Commodus, AD 180–192, Mithraism had become one of the foremost state cults, a position it held for a long time.

Roman Mithraism bears striking resemblances to, and remarkable differences from, the Persian worship of Mithra. That there should be differences is only natural, for in moving into the Roman world the cult was subject to a whole new range of influences and ideas. Worshippers coming to Mithraism from a Hellenistic or Egyptian cult, of which there were many in the second century AD, would naturally bring with them the richness of their various backgrounds. One of the most striking differences is the fact that for Roman Mithraism there are virtually no texts but hundreds of reliefs, whereas for Persia there is only one relief and many texts. It is very difficult to present a belief, particularly an abstract concept, in stone and it may be that Roman Mithraism had a more abstract mythology than we realise.

The Roman reliefs are generally interpreted as depicting a primeval life of Mithras. He was, it is said, born from a rock as a youth, not as a child, bearing the emblems of his office: the dagger with which he will one day slay the bull, a torch symbolising the light entering the world and sometimes an orb symbolising his cosmic rule. His birth was attended either by the two torch-bearers, Cautes and Cautapates, or by shepherds with their flock. On one occasion, in response to the prayers of his followers, he shot an arrow into a rock, thereby producing water for his thirsting followers. A number of reliefs show Mithras riding forth to the hunt on his horse accompanied by a snake and a lion. Some small panels show the heads of Mithras and his companions in a tree, presumably hiding. The main scenes depict the god's adventures with the bull. Before he can slay the bull he has to catch it, a task which proves extremely difficult. Mithras first caught the bull while it was grazing, but the bull broke free and

Two Kushana representations of Miiro (Mithra). In both he is shown with a radiate crown, and wearing tunic, mantle and short boots. In the first he carries a staff and holds out his hand, perhaps in blessing; in the second he carries a sword and torque.

right *Virtually every Mithraeum had a bull-slaying scene as its central relief. The god is shown sacrificing the bull in a cave, represented by the stylised arch with leaf ornament, while various members of creation (dog, snake and scorpion) partake of life at its source. The life-giving character of this cosmic sacrifice (notice the busts of the sun and moon) is symbolised by the wheat springing from the bull's tail. Two interesting details of this particular relief are the triangular niches over the heads of the torch-bearers, in which lamps were placed, and the evidence for the original use of paint on the relief: red for the god's clothes and the busts of the sun and moon and black for the bull.*

below *The Mithraic communion meal scene from a relief at Konjic in Yugoslavia. Sol and Mithras, reclining behind a table draped with a bull skin, are attended by worshippers wearing the masks of their grade within the mysteries (see pages 86–7). In the foreground is a table with four loaves for the ritual meal, each bearing the sign of a cross. These markings may have had a practical value—they helped to break the bread—and a symbolic significance, for the cross is an old symbol for the sun. The meal is celebrated in a cave symbolising the cosmos.*

left *A Mithraic communion meal scene dated c. AD 140 discovered at Ladenburgh by Dr B. Heukemes in 1965. This relief, together with the associated finds, will be published when permission has been granted to complete excavations of the surrounding land and the Mithraeum. The relief (height 1·40 m., width 1·50 m. depth 0·30 m.), was originally painted. The author is heavily indebted to Dr Heukemes for being allowed to publish the first picture of this significant relief. The scene shows Mithras and Sol with drinking cups reclining on a couch draped with a bull skin behind a table with bulls' legs on which fruit is set. The stylised arch appears to represent a cave.*

below *A large relief of Mithra from Arsameia in Commagene. The part of the relief showing the king, with whom Mithra was shaking hands, is now missing, but it was presumably Mithradates Kallinikos. The handshake is an important part of Persian ritual.*

dragged the god along behind it until at last the beast was exhausted and Mithras was able to take it back to the cave to slay it. The slaying of the bull is usually taken as an act of creation. The forces of good (represented by the dog) and the forces of evil (represented by the snake and the scorpion) fought over the source of life, the life-giving blood and seed of the bull. But the victory of good is assured for life, in the shape of corn, springing from the tail of the moribund victim. Finally, before his ascent to heaven Mithras shared a communion meal with Sol, a meal celebrated over the body of the bull and one which is re-enacted by the faithful in their rituals.

Although this is the interpretation of Mithraic mythology which is given in almost all the books, it is very questionable. Some of the details do not bear close scrutiny. The argument that the dog and snake are fighting on the bull-slaying scenes, for example, is a dubious interpretation of the reliefs. One may doubt if the snake really symbolises evil, for on the hunting scenes the snake runs alongside Mithras as his companion. The idea that the three heads in a tree represent Mithras and his companions hiding is very speculative, perhaps rather humourous! But more than this one may doubt the whole theory of a life of Mithras. Hellenic religions may have told stories about the lives of their gods, but the Persians did not. We have seen again and again in this book that the Persians used mythical imagery (rather than mythical narratives) simply to give expression to abstract concepts, and although there was Hellenic influence on Mithraism the introduction of the life of a god is such a fundamental change that one may doubt if it ever occurred. Instead, perhaps we should take the various scenes as the expressions of abstract concepts. The archer producing water, for example, rather than portraying an event in the life of the god, a sort of 'Mithraic Moses', perhaps represents a belief in Mithras as the bestower of rain as in Indo-Iranian belief, the arrow representing lightning and storm, the source of fertility. The scene would then not represent an isolated incident, but would stand as a symbol of the continual work of the god as the giver of life. The hunting scenes should perhaps be seen as picture images of the god charging into the world hunting out all who oppose the truth and not simply as a 'jolly day in the forest'!

In the last analysis we cannot say for certain which of the two approaches is

top right *An ordeal pit at the rear of the Carrawburgh Mithraeum near Newcastle. Such coffin-shaped pits have been found in other Mithraea. They were used as places for testing the initiate. Perhaps there was something of the idea of dying to the old life and rising to the new at initiation.*

below right *Much research enabled this full-scale colour reconstruction of Carrawburgh Mithraeum at Newcastle upon Tyne. After entering the 'ante-chapel' with its ordeal pit, the worshipper passed down the central aisle flanked by statues representing the setting and rising sun (hence the lowered and raised torches), between benches whereon the faithful reclined for the communion meal, to stand before the three main altars and central relief. The temple was lit and constructed to look like the cosmic cave in which the god slew the bull which is the source of all life. This creative and redemptive act, portrayed on the relief, is attended by the twins, the rising and setting sun, while heavenly bodies look on and the dog and snake leap to receive the shed eternal blood.*

below *Two scenes from the Mithraeum at Tabernae. In the top scene Mithras' birth from the rock is attended by shepherds with their flock. In the bottom Mithras, in answer to the prayers of a worshipper, shoots an arrow into a rock and produces life-giving water. It may be that the shepherd motif is due to Christian influence.*

the correct one. But the reader should be warned that what can at first sight appear to be a simple, factual re-telling of a myth can in fact be a tendentious interpretation or even sheer guess-work. This is particularly true in the case of Roman Mithraism. The problems involved in reconstructing Mithraic mythology can best be illustrated by looking at the figure of the lion-headed god, statues of which appear in many Mithraic temples. Some scholars believe that this represents Ahriman, the devil of Zoroastrianism. They point out that inscriptions have been found in Mithraic temples to Ahrimanius, and the horrific character of the statue supports this. But others believe this statue to be a representation of Zurvan, the Absolute Being, the father of good and evil. The horrific character of the statue is accounted for by the idea of all-consuming Time, and these scholars would support their arguments by pointing out that there are some lion-headed figures with pleasant appearances, which is rather surprising if the figure is the devil. Whatever the rights and wrongs of these arguments, when it is difficult to decide whether a figure represents the high god or the devil, then one has to show very great caution in trying to reconstruct the mythology of the cult!

But whatever the problems of reconstructing Mithraic mythology Mithra remains a god whose worship spans many centuries and many countries. We do not know if he was ever worshipped in a separate and distinct cult in ancient Persia, but we do know that today he is a very popular figure in Zoroastrianism. The village shrines to Mithra in Persia are visited by the faithful on feast days, and there they kindle fires, light candles and make small offerings during their prayers to the great Yazata, the preserver of Truth and Order, the enemy of the Lie and the destroyer of Falsehood.

1

2

4

6

1 Initiates in the cult of Mithraism were divided into seven grades of ascending order. The different grades appear to have symbolised the ascent of the soul through the heavens. The symbol of the first grade was that of the raven. According to Jerome members of this grade wore a raven's mask, which explains the figure on the left of the Konjic communion meal relief (page 82).

2 The symbol of the second grade is that of the bride, the initiate who was wedded to the cult. He wore a short yellow tunic with red bands and was thought to stand under the protection of Venus.

3 The third grade was that of the soldier. On initiation to this grade the initiate had to kneel naked and blindfolded. A crown was offered to him on a sword, which he rejected, having no crown but Mithras. The idea of the god and believer as warriors on behalf of truth was dominant in Indian and Persian belief.

4 The fourth grade, of the lion, was the first of the higher grades. The Konjic relief (page 82) suggests that members of this grade wore an animal mask at the communion meal. In other reliefs they simply attend in distinctive red tunics with purple stripes. The lion's symbol incorporates a thunderbolt and fire shovel, for having entered the grade of fire it was the lion who attended the sacred altar flame. The third element in his symbol is an Egyptian metal rattle, often used in the mystery cults.

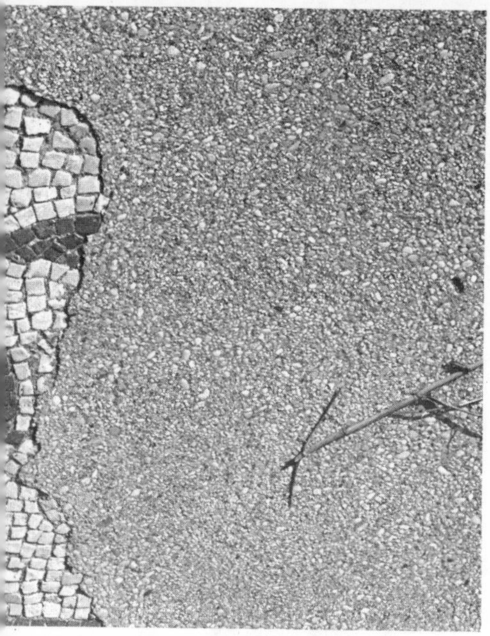

3

5 On entry to the grade of lion and to the sixth grade of Persian the initiate was purified with honey. The symbols of the Persian are ears of corn and a sickle, for he is said to be 'the keeper of the fruits' (Porphyry).

6 The courier of the sun had as his symbols some of the attributes of Sol–the radiate crown, torch and whip. Initiates of this grade took the place of Sol at the communion meal.

7 The father, or seventh grade, was the earthly representative of Mithras. He took the god's place at the communion meal and was responsible for the discipline and teaching of the faithful. The ring and staff in the symbol indicate his role as teacher, the Persian cap shows his relation to the god. He also had the sickle of Saturn.

5

7

This mosaic of the magi from San Apollinare Nuovo in Ravenna is so accurate in its depiction of Parthian dress (the cloak, coat and trousers) that some scholars have suggested the Christian artist knew of a Mithraic scene in which magi brought gifts to the newly born saviour.

+SCS MELCHIOR +SCS GASPAR

MYTH AND THE PROPHET

Zoroaster was a historical figure, a man born at a particular place at a particular time, even though we do not know for certain where or when. His hymns, the *Gathas,* are personal compositions with the clear ring of authenticity. The rise of Zoroastrianism cannot be understood without accepting the existence of such a person. The purpose of this chapter is not to undermine the historicity of the figure, but to see how, as with all religions, the stories of the founder's work have been adapted and developed by his followers. The faithful have a need to visualise the founder clearly 'and have therefore unconsciously added to the accounts handed down to them the details that did this for them. It will be well if the reader says to himself: "Here is the story that millions have taken for truth, *and they have also lived by it; but* the historians are very doubtful of its accuracy"' (*Noss, p. 156, n.*) In trying to understand what a prophet means to his followers the developed myth or legend can be of greater help than a purely scholarly reconstruction of history.

For the Greeks Zoroaster was the archetypal magus or priest, the great Persian sage. Plato is said to have wanted to travel to the Orient and learn from his 'pupils', the magi. There is even a tradition that Socrates had a magus for a teacher. Many famous Greeks, including Aristotle, knew the Persian teachings, and a number of books apparently circulated throughout the Greek world under the name of Zoroaster. The Greeks placed Zoroaster in hoary antiquity, dating him six thousand years before Plato, an adaptation and misunderstanding of the Zoroastrian scheme of history. Such awe for the ancient oriental sage must, of course, derive ultimately from the Persian attitude to the prophet, but this is not mythology; for that we have to look at the beliefs surrounding the life of the teacher of the Good Religion.

The coming of Zoroaster, it is believed, was foretold to a number of holy beings. It was first told to the primeval ox who had been slain by Ahriman when he first attacked the world. The soul of the ox protested to the creator that it had no protector in the world of creatures. When it was shown the heavenly self, or fravashi, of Zoroaster who would come to protect the species, then the ox was satisfied and consented to return to earth to nourish mankind. The coming of Zoroaster was also foretold to Yima in the paradisal age. A patriarchal king, the prince Us, was told of the coming of Zoroaster by

Clouds gathering over the ruins at Persepolis.

the ox and in one of the ancient *Yashts* it is said that the Divine Glory had been passed from saint to saint so that it could illumine the soul of Zoroaster. Thus Zoroaster, to the Zoroastrian, is no historical accident. Not only is he the turning point of history, his birth marking the beginning of the millennium when evil would be defeated, but he is also the foreordained turning point of history to which creation has looked since Ahriman first attacked the world.

Zoroaster was not conceived in the ordinary way, but from the Divine Glory passing through the heavens to the earth where it united itself with a girl of fifteen, the ideal age in Persian thought. The glory residing within her filled her with such splendour that her father, misguided by the demons, assumed she was bewitched and sent her away from home. It was only then that she married. Zoroaster's spirit was conveyed to the mother through the stem of the haoma plant by the archangels. His material form was mixed with haoma and milk by another two archangels and drunk by the parents, despite the frenzied attempts of the demons to destroy it. To the Zoroastrians, then, while Zoroaster is a man and ever remains such, he is not simply as other men are, his birth was miraculous and the work of the divine.

At the birth of Zoroaster all the creatures of the Good Creation, the plants and the waters, rejoiced, but the demons were terror-struck. They knew that where the gods had failed to smite them, Zoroaster could. The birth of the prophet was an answer to the prayers and offerings of haoma by his father; it was also a remarkable birth. As soon as he was brought forth he laughed, a light shone around the house, and most significant of all, from the moment of birth he was able to converse with Ohrmazd. Conscious of his mission from the first, Zoroaster declared himself a worshipper of Ohrmazd.

Like so many of the great religious teachers, Zoroaster is believed to have been the object of demonic attempts to destroy or seduce him. A wizard tried to crush the head of the young child and on another occasion the forces of evil tried to destroy him by fire. Again, a herd of oxen stampeded down a narrow path towards the child, but the leading ox stood guard over Zoroaster, preserving him from death. The attempts to destroy him continued by sorcery, by treachery and by dispute, but all were in vain, foiled either by divine intervention or because Zoroaster, like the young Jesus, was able to confound the teachings of the elders. A series of stories are told illuminating the compassion of the young prophet for animals. There are stories, too, about his leaving home, living in silence and meditating in the desert. So, from before the day of his birth the conflict with evil began. The millennium in which evil would be defeated had dawned. Fight as they might the end of the demons was assured.

At the age of thirty Zoroaster received his first vision. One day as he was fetching pure water from a river for the haoma pressing, he had a premonition of the vision which was to be given him. Then before him he saw a transcendent figure of enormous proportions. After laying aside his body he was transported into the presence of the angels, where he took a seat among the enquirers in heaven and was instructed in the Good Religion. This was the first of eight visions Zoroaster had of God and his Good Mind. Thus through Zoroaster there is a direct communication to man of the Truth from heaven. Zoroaster through his personal experience of God was able to reveal to man the will of the divine.

His teaching was rejected at first. Men were hard of heart and Zoroaster needed the comfort of God. After the period of visions was over and the revelation complete, he was tempted by the demons, who sought to destroy him, to persuade him to worship them and to destroy the faith with false visions. But all was in vain. Zoroaster was resolute in the faith, steadfast in the recital of the sacred prayers and faithful in his practice of the Zoroastrian rituals. He stands as the true model and guide for all his followers in the trials and temptations that beset them.

As in most religious traditions, the Zoroastrians believe that the hand of God was at work in the ministry of the great prophet, particularly in the early conversions. Followers are drawn by the manifestations of God in the miraculous work of the teacher. When Zoroaster had made his first converts, guided by God, he visited the palace of the king, Vishtaspa, that he might convert him also. The royal court was a home of superstition, magic and suspicion. The learned men of the court disputed with Zoroaster for three whole days but as the prophet's ability to know the king's thoughts was impressing Vishtaspa, the wicked and jealous priests hatched a plot against him and Zoroaster was cast into prison as a necromancer. Then a miracle occurred: the king's favourite black horse grew ill and its legs drew up into its body so that it could not move. Zoroaster offered to restore the horse to its full health on the granting of four conditions. The first was that the king should accept the faith; the second was that the warlike prince, Isfandiyar, should fight for the Good Religion; the third was that the queen should accept the Good Religion, and the fourth was that the names of the plotters must be revealed. As each condition was granted one of the horse's legs was restored until the horse returned to perfect health and vigour.

After his conversion Vishtaspa asked that he might know his place in heaven, whereupon three archangels appeared at the monarch's court. Their glory filled the palace so that the king and his courtiers trembled, but their fears were calmed for the protective presence of God at court was promised and victory over their foes assured. The king was granted his petition for a vision of his place in heaven, and his son, Peshyotan, was given immortality. Isfandiyar was made invulnerable in the defence of the Good Religion, and the Grand Vizier was given universal wisdom. The court was thus converted and the victorious march of the Zoroastrian faith began. With the aid of God the Good Religion was given the support of an earthly king, the heavenly teaching became available to men and the miraculous powers of the prophet were made manifest.

A Parsi decorating a representation of the prophet, Zoroaster.

دین وملت او شدند واز معجزات او یکی آن بود که پارهٔ آتش در دست داشت ودستش نمی سوخت چون گشتاسف مجلس او درآمد
بدست گشتاسف داد دستش نسوخت وهرکه دران مجلس بود که از دست زردشت بدست گرفتند دستشان نسوخت این اثر دعم گبران
آن است که آتشی که دارند از آن آتش است وهرگز از آن وقت باز فرو نشسته است وبعضی گویند گشتاسف در ابتدا دین او قبول نکرد وبفرمود
تا او را بزندان کردند ومدت هفت سال در زندان بود روزی گشتاسف سوار بود هر چهار دست وپای اسبش در شکم فرو رفت
وهیچ اثر از دست وپا پیدا نبود ومردم همه متحیر گشتند که این چه سرّ است گشتاسف زردشت را طلب فرمود وسنت این قصیه از او پرسید
او گفت سبب آنست که فرمان من که پیغمبرم نمی بری اکنون اگر فرمان من خواهی برد من دعا کنم تا خدای تعالی دست وپای او بدو باز دهد
گشتاسف قبول کرد که اگر او دست وپای اسب پیدا کند گشتاسف بدو ایمان آورد وزردشت دعا کرد دست وپای او همان
قرار اول رفت وکوری در دنور بود زردشت برو بگذشت وگیاهی بدو نشان داد که آنرا در چشم کش تا چشمت روشن
شود چنان کرد وچشمش روشن شد وآن نیز گفته اند که زر بروی گداختند ودر وهیچ اثر نکرد وگفته اند مس را برو گداختند

با طلا شد وملالی بدو نرسید وگشتاسف بدین او درآمد ومدد او کرد واو شریعتی نهاد که موافق اخلاق گشتاسف بود و
کتاب خود را ابستاق میخواند وان بلغتی بود که هیچ کس فهم نمی کرد وگویند لغات آن کتاب را سصت حرف است
ودر هیچ لغت این قدر حرف نیست وزردشت میگفت من از حضرت آن مبعوث شده ام که این کتاب بر شما بخوانم که این سخن

Naturally, legends have grown up about the king, the court and Zoroaster's ter life and about missionary work in distant lands, but these clearly belong to e category of legend and indicate little of the position of the prophet in the ythology of Zoroastrianism, unlike the birth, vision and conversion nar- tives, which through their religious significance can be classed as myth.

Regarding the death of Zoroaster the Persian tradition is unanimous in tributing it to the hand of a murderer. Aged seventy-seven, the prophet was lled while in the sanctuary. The Persian sources give few details and there is othing suggestive of myth or legend about them. A mythical form is, how- ver, given by Christian writers. This represents a deliberate attempt to bring oroaster into disrepute, and provides a good example of the way in which yth can be used to bring discredit to an opponent. The source behind the any versions which exist seems to be the Clementine *Recognitions*. Zoroaster identified with Ham, the son of Noah, and to deceive people he used to onjure up the stars until a presiding genie, angry at his control, destroyed oroaster, the arch-magician, with fire from heaven. The Persians, ever fools, ified the ashes and praised the star which they claimed transported Zoroaster to the presence of God. This is said to explain the form of his name, 'Zoro' is ken as the Greek for life, 'aster' the Greek for star, hence 'the living star'. The rly Christians, in common with many religious traditions, were quite good 'mud-slinging'.

From various sources we have been able to reconstruct something of the ythical development of the figure of Zoroaster. The dating of this develop- ent is very difficult, and for present purposes totally unnecessary. These yths show how the historical figure of Zoroaster was understood by the ithful, and what he meant to them as their great religious teacher. He is their eal man, the one who revealed the will of God to man, the one who com- unicated with God, the one who wrought fear in the hearts of evil forces and ho, on the human scale, is chiefly responsible for their destruction. In these yths one can see the projection of the great cosmic battles into the life of the rson who may be called the archetypal Zoroastrian. The fact that he is the ithority for many of their rituals should not be interpreted, as it has been by me scholars, as evidence that he is a cultic creation. This is a natural religious ndency, just as Christians trace the history of the Eucharist back to the life d actions of Jesus. As the first Zoroastrian priest and missionary it is inevitable at Zoroaster should be viewed as the inspiration of the Zoroastrian religious fe. Equally natural is the idea that all three social classes, priest, warrior and isbandman, should be contained in his being, for what great saviour could eglect a major body of society. Some have asked whether Zoroaster is ought of as a god or man in the myths. This is an unnecessary question. lthough he is said to be more effective than all the Yazatas in defeating evil is is only because Ohrmazd has chosen him as the vessel to bear the Good eligion into the world. Zoroaster is often presented talking to Ohrmazd and e faithful revere the great teacher, but Zoroaster forever remains man, hrmazd the sovereign Lord.

The just king Gushtasp (Vishtaspa) on his throne with his gallant brother, Zarir, his son, the valiant warrior, Isfandiyar, receiving instruction from Zoroaster. According to the Shah name *Gushtasp established fire temples and spread the radiance of God throughout the realm.*

MYTH AND THE KING

In the ancient Near East the king was often thought of as divine and his person and function were surrounded by myth. In this section we shall look at Persian belief to see if a similar pattern presents itself there.

In these days of central heating and refrigeration it is difficult for many of us to understand the ancient sense of complete dependence on the regularity of the seasons. In Egypt the sequence of the seasons was quite regular, but this was far from being so in Mesopotamia. There life was insecure and men believed that unless they could participate in the cosmic events survival could not be guaranteed. A mediator between man and the gods was needed and, they believed, supplied in the person of the king.

It is well known that the ancient Egyptians believed the king to be divine, the son of Re, the source of stability and security. In Mesopotamia there was a similar idea, but with important differences. There the king was not the physical offspring of the gods, but on the day of his accession to the throne he became the adopted son of god and he henceforth acted as god on earth and represented the people before the gods. One of his primary tasks was to ensure the proper sequence of the seasons so that his flock might live. The ordering of the seasons was achieved through an annual ritual, the New Year Festival, in which the king, taking the part of the god, re-enacted the primeval battle whereby god had defeated the forces of chaos in the shape of a monster, and had produced order in the world. This drama was not just a symbol of what *had* happened, it was also an effective source which ensured that the same creative order would be released in the coming year so that life would again triumph over the forces of chaos.

Persia bordered on Mesopotamia and had many close contacts with her; how far did the Persians take over this belief and practice?

In Persian thought there are two instruments of the forces of good in their combat with evil, the brothers of religion and kingship. The two co-exist but do not coincide. Obedience to the king and knowledge of the Good Religion are the two factors necessary to the defeat of evil. In an ideal state 'Religion is royalty, and royalty is Religion' (*Dk.M.47:6, ZDT, p. 296*). Anarchy is, fundamentally, a product of evil religion. The good king manifests the Bounteous Spirit of God and is a symbol of his sovereignty on earth. It is his

On this rock relief from Naqsh-i Rustam Ohrmazd (right) offers the diadem and gift of kingship to Ardashir I (224–241 AD). The king is not presented as smaller than the god, nor as bending the knee before him, indeed his crown stands higher than that of Ohrmazd. Just as Ohrmazd tramples on the head of the devil, Ahriman (note the snake in the devil's head-dress), so Ardashir tramples on Ardavan, the last Parthian king. Ohrmazd is shown holding the barsom, the symbol of his priestly person.

above *One of a number of reliefs at Persepolis showing a lion attacking a bull. The theme is so common that a mythical interpretation has been proposed suggesting that the battle represents the struggle of the seasons.*

left *Ardashir II (AD 379–383) is shown receiving the crown from Ohrmazd (on the right). On the left is Mithra, with a crown composed of the rays of the sun, holding the sacred barsom and standing on a lotus plant, a sacred symbol. While Mithra thus appears in a priestly role Ardashir II and Ohrmazd stand like conquering heroes on the body of a vanquished enemy. A relief from Taq-i Bustan.*

far left *A relief from Naqsh-i Rustam of the third or fourth century AD showing the goddess Anahita (on the right) investing the king Narseh with the symbol of kingship. The very ornate style used on this relief can also be seen on a number of Sasanian coins. The rippling effect on the goddess' clothes may be intended to recall her character as goddess of the waters.*

right *A detail from the relief above the tomb of Artaxerxes (fourth century BC). The imitation of the tomb of Darius is obvious. The king is shown praying before the eternal fire in the presence of God, depicted by the famous winged symbol.*

far right *The tomb of the great Darius at Naqsh-i Rustam. The spot was marked as a sacred site by an ancient Elamite relief. On the large rock face a number of reliefs were carved; two smaller Sasanian reliefs can be seen in this photograph under the tomb of Darius. The front of the tomb is in the shape of a cross, possibly a deliberately selected symbolic shape.*

A cylinder seal impression of Darius. The inscription records his name in old Persian, Elamite and Babylonian. The king, under the protection of Ahura Mazda, does battle with raging lions. One lion rising on his hind legs like a demonic being recalls the style of the Ziwiye figures (pages 28–9).

duty to expand the creation, the Good Religion and the happiness of his subjects, for these are the manifestations of God's desires for mankind. Although the Good Religion was first propounded in Persia it is essentially a message for all mankind.

In Persian mythology the ideal king was thought to be Yima, and Nauruz, the festival instigated by Yima, is the Persian New Year Festival. In the Sasanian period kings were definitely thought of as divine; they were said to be the brothers of the sun and moon and were called gods. On a number of reliefs it is Ohrmazd himself who invests them with the insignia of kingship and their crowns bear the symbols of the different gods. The supernatural character of the kings is indicated on a number of reliefs by the presence of a halo, the Divine Glory. The great king Khusrau depicted himself enthroned in heaven surrounded by the stars. Thus there is little doubt of the divine character of the Sasanian kings.

What of the earlier period and what mythological significance and functions were attached to this position? Here the question is much more difficult to answer, but in view of the contact of Persia with other nations and the deployment of foreign labour it would be surprising if some influence were not felt. When Cyrus the Great (559–530 BC) ruled Babylonia he had his son, Cambyses, installed as king of Mesopotamia according to the traditional Babylonian manner at the New Year Festival in 538. Cyrus wished to make his son acceptable to the Babylonians by having him installed with a ceremony of approval and adoption by their god Marduk. The same prince was presented in Egypt as son of the Egyptian god Re. Naturally one wonders if these actions reflected or influenced the Persian idea of kingship.

Cambyses is not the only figure for whom we have suggestions of the idea of sacred kingship. Darius (522–486 BC) was largely responsible for the construction of a magnificent palace at Persepolis in south-west Persia. The size, beauty and magnificence of this city is hard to describe. Covering an enormous area, huge buildings were erected with a wealth of detailed reliefs and carvings, a work which we know took many years. Yet the palace was rarely used. Among the remains there is little or nothing to suggest that it was ever used for administrative purposes. Persepolis appears rather as a ritual centre, the scene

This relief of a hunting scene is on the wall of the main iwan *at Taq-i Bustan and probably comes from the time of Khusrau II (AD 590–628). The elephant riders on the left drive the boar into the swamps on which the king of kings sails in his boat. In the centre the king is shown shooting the boar, on the right the boar is seen dead. The movement of the animals from left to right carries the eye from one scene to the next. Artistically the patterns of the animals and reeds is very pleasant. Theologically the scene is interesting for the picture of the king. His importance is stressed not only by his size and dominance of the centre relief, but also by the halo which surrounds his head symbolising the presence of the divine glory, or* hvarenah.

The exterior of Darius' palace at Susa was decorated with multi-coloured glazed bricks, giving a wonderfully delicate effect. These two scenes show a pair of winged genii beneath the winged symbol of Ahura Mazda, and one of the famous lion-griffins. They are yet another example of motifs taken over from Babylon.

far right *Shapur III (AD 383–388) receiving the crown from his father, Shapur II, stressing the legitimacy of one who had had to fight for the throne. The magnificent king in armour underneath probably dates from the reign of Khusrau II (AD 590–628). The Persians were noted for the strength of their armour, which is illustrated in minute detail on this relief.*

of the annual festival where the peoples of the empire gathered to pay their dues and tokens of loyalty to the king of kings. Processions passed up a staircase so constructed that a horse could be ridden up it, through gate-houses into a hall of a hundred columns–which, it has been suggested, resembled the sacred grove–past crenellated walls symbolising the sacred mountain. These processions were not merely ostentatious displays of wealth but displays before God of the fruitfulness of the land. The Nauruz festival has further connections with the seasons, for it coincides with the feast of Rapithwin (see pp.), the time when prayer is offered for the return of the god from his hiding place in the earth where he has kept alive the roots of the plants despite the onslaughts of winter. The battle of the seasons may be symbolised in some reliefs which show a lion (the sun) slaying a bull (the rains). The reliefs at Persepolis, therefore, suggest that there was an annual festival in Persia which was associated with the struggle of the seasons and forces of life.

The king's role in all this is not clear. In their many inscriptions the kings present themselves as completely dependent on Ahura Mazda. It is Ahura Mazda who makes them king, who gives them strength, who protects them, their lands and all they do. But it is the kings who make effective the will of god on earth. Darius in an inscription at Susa proclaims that he copies the work of God for he, like God, makes the world excellent (*frasha*):

By the grace of Ahura Mazda I have done this, that which I have done appears *frasha* to the whole world.
Kent, p. 141

Shapur II (AD 309–79) hunting lions, a scene from a bowl of the fourth century AD. The king is shown employing the famous 'Parthian shot', turning and shooting over the shoulder while galloping away.

On the reliefs the kings are represented under the hovering winged symbol of Ahura Mazda, fairly clear signs that they represent God on earth. Did they take part in a ritual battle with the powers of evil as in Babylonia? We do not know. There are a number of reliefs and seals on which the king is shown fighting with a monster. The style of the seals suggests Babylonian influence and again one wonders if it was only the outward art form which was taken over.

Some scholars have gone much further than this and suggested that the king was thought of as the incarnation of Mithra and that on his accession to the throne he dramatically re-enacted the birth of Mithra in a cave. It has also been suggested that the king played the part of the dragon-slaying Thraetaona in a ritual drama. But the evidence for these theories is so slight and complex that we must leave them on one side.

In later times at least then, the Persian king was thought of as divine. He was the essential complement to the priest, for religion and kingship are brothers. His archetype was Yima, the primeval king who ruled in peace, expanded the world, but fought no battles. If the ancient Persians took over anything of the Babylonian concept of the king it does not appear that they thought of him as the son of God, but rather as God's special representative, working under his protection. He was himself so exalted that his face was masked before the people, his presence concealed behind a curtain and ordinary men prostrated themselves before him. Perhaps to the ordinary people the great king of kings was more than man and the masses may even in early times have seen in him the present manifestation of the legendary kings who slew dragons and ruled over demons. To the king and the priests the royal role was to overcome the disruptive forces at work within the empire. When rebels arose, to use the words of the great Darius himself, it was 'the Lie that made them rebellious'. The great cosmic battle between the Truth and the Lie was a battle in which the king was engaged, but the emphasis seems to have been on his role in establishing the order and peace of God's kingdom in his own realm with the aid of the Wise Lord rather than on a ritual ordering of the seasons, though the one need not exclude the other. The Persians could not have been unaware of the Babylonian myths of kingship, but they appear to have transferred myth into history and in their mythical symbols expressed their conviction that the good king manifests the Bounteous Spirit of God. They looked for the day when perfect kingship would combine with the Good Religion, for then the renovation would occur.

above *The Cyrus cylinder from Babylon is a contemporary record by Cyrus of his policy towards subject peoples after his capture of Nineveh. He ordered the restoration of temples and deported peoples. It was as a result of this edict that the faithful of the Jewish exiles in Babylon returned to Israel and began to rebuild the temple.*

right *A scene from the hall of a hundred columns at Persepolis showing a hero (the king?) fighting a monster. As the Babylonian monarchs enacted the battle of the gods with monsters one might ask if this scene at the 'ritual city' of Persepolis implies a similar belief concerning the Persian kings.*

These two details from the stairway at Persepolis give a clear picture of the beautiful simplicity of the carvings. It is thought by some that the battle between the lion and the bull was a symbol for the battle between the seasons: summer (the lion) devouring the rains (the bull). At great annual festivals bearers of tribute from all parts of the empire processed up the steps and into the presence of the king of kings, the stairway being so constructed that horses could be ridden up it. The crenellated walls are thought to symbolise the sacred mountain, and the many trees either the mythological world tree or the sacred grove. The palace has many symbolic as well as many magnificent features.

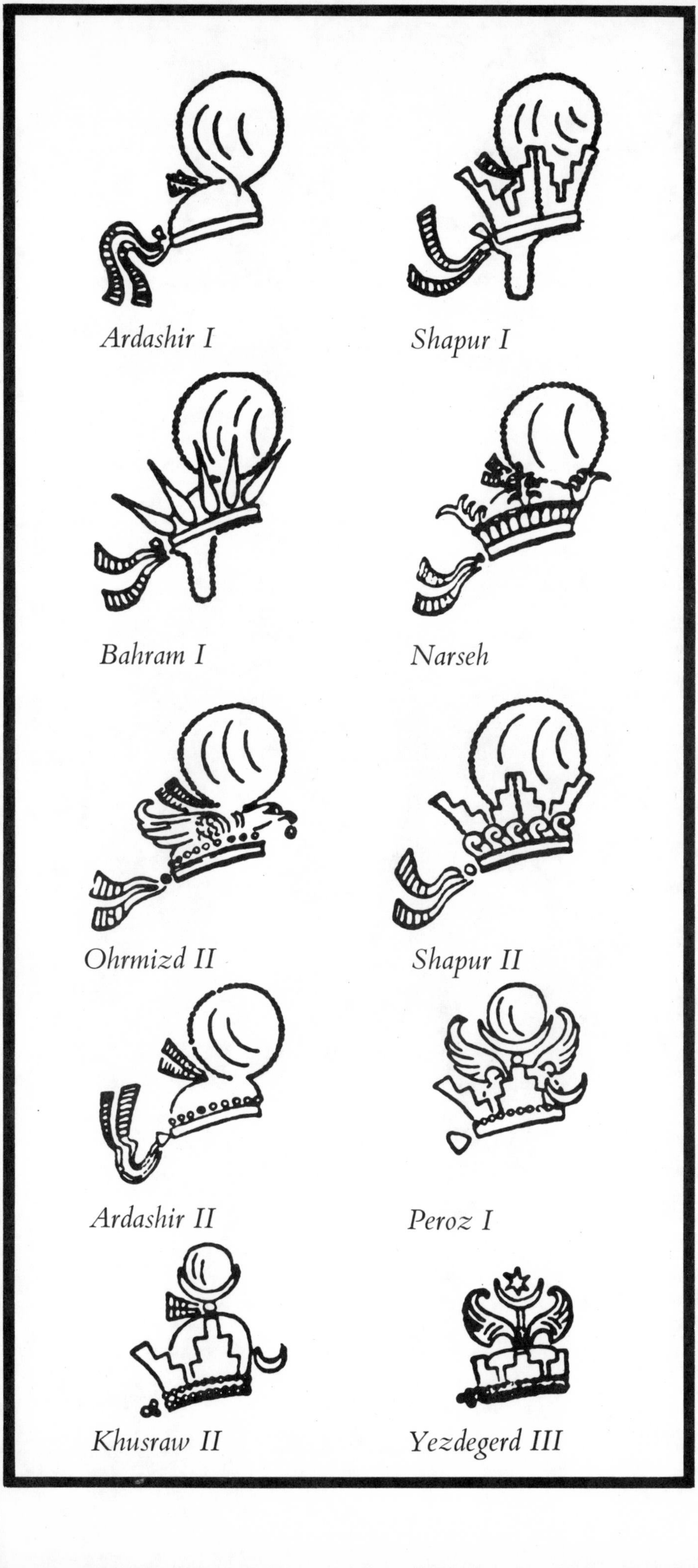

The crowns worn by the Sasanian kings embodied the symbols of different gods. The battlements on those of Shapur I and II may be derived from Achaemenid styles; the rays on the crown of Bahram I are from the symbol for Mithra; the leaves on Narseh's crown have been ascribed to Anahita; the wings and eagle's head on the crown of Hohrmizd II may symbolise Verethraghna, the god of victory. Peroz I, Khusrau II and Yezdegerd III employed the symbol of the Moon god, Mah. The royal crown was so heavy that it could not rest on the king's head but was suspended from the ceiling over the throne.

ذکر کیومرث

مورخ که تاریخ عالم نهاد	ز گفتار دهقان چنین کرد یاد	که تا کرد بنیاد گیتی خدای	ز شاهان با فر و فرهنگ و رای
نخستین خدیوی که کشور گشود	سر نامداران کیومرث بود	چو بنشست بر تخت و بنهاد تاج	بینداخت بر مرد دهقان خراج

بداد و دهش خلق را وعده کرد جهان را بنام نکو عهد کرد راویان آثار از آن پادشاه کامکار اخبار چنین کرده‌اند
که کیومرث از اسباط مهلائیل بود و در بحر الانساب فرزند صلبی آدم نبشته است و امام حجة الاسلام محمد بن محمد الغزالی رحمه الله
در کتاب نصیحة الملوک آورده است که کیومرث برادر شیث بود و بعضی گویند از اولاد نوح است و در زعم طایفه‌ای از مغان
کیومرث خود آدم است علی الجمله تا اختلاف انساب اتفاق دارند که نخستین پادشاهی است از پادشاهان جهان و معنی کیومرث
بلغت سریانی حی ناطق است یعنی زنده گویا و بحقیقت اسم او با مسمی مطابقتی دارد با وجود بسطت ملک و کثرت سپاه و نفاذ
امر مشعوف بود بسیاحت و منازل و مراحل در تحت قدم آوردن و شهاکرد کوه و دشت گشتن و بر خرابه و سواحل گذشتن
و چون از تدبیر ملک و مصالح رغبت بپرداختی در شعاف مهاوی مهیب و شعاب شوامخ عظیم ماوا ساختی و شبها و روزها
بنوحه و عبادت گذرانیدی چون رقاب گردنکشان در ربقه عهد و پیمان و طوق عبودیت و فرمان آورد با دیوان و مرده و عفاریت شیاطین محاربات کرد
و سلاح او چوب و فلاخن بود و لباس او از پوست پلنگ و علماء تواریخ اکثری چنین گویند که دیو و پری در اوایل بنی آدم آشکارا بودند و یکدیگر را دیدندی

و دوستی و دشمنی و حرب با دیوان ظاهر بودی تا بوقت نوح بعد از طوفان بر خلق ناپدید شدند و در ایام کیومرث لباس آدمیان از جلود
حیوانات بود و مردمان از دیوان در زحمت بودند او خلایق را از ظلم ایشان خلاص داد و دیوان را از آبادانیها براند و جناح عدل
و احسان بر سر بنی آدم بگسترد و در کشف ظلمات متظلمان و قضاء حوایج ملهوفان زمینا لعب نمود و گفت انا ملک الارض بامر الله
من پادشاه زمین و نگاه دارنده خلقانم بفرمان خدای تعالی و لقب او گلشاه بود نشستن گاه خود نزدیک دماوند ساخت
و بغایت خوب صورت بود و با فر او راد و فرزند آمد مشی و مشانه نام نهاد مشی مذکر و مشانه مونث و بعضی گویند هوشنگ
اول فرزند اوست و مشی بغایت زاهد و متعبد بود روزی از پدر پرسید که از کارها چه بهتر پدرش گفت کم آزاری
مردمان و پرستش خدای عز و جل هوشنگ گفت که بی آزاری نتوان بود مگر جدا بودن از ایشان و طاعت نتوان کرد مگر شبها و بدین
سبب از خلایق کرانه گرفت و در کوه بسر می برد گاهی پدر بدیدن او رفتی و گاهی او بدیدن پدر آمدی پس گروهی از آن

MYTH AND HISTORY

Myth as an Interpretation of History

In once sense all myth is part of history, for myth embodies the views of man about himself, his world and its development. This is particularly true of the myths of the Persians, for their myths of creation and the renovation are interpretations of, or reflections upon, the process of world history. As we have seen they divided world history into four periods, each of three thousand years. The first two periods are concerned with creation, the third is the period when the wills of Ormazd and Ahriman are mixed in the world, and the fourth period is the time when evil will be overcome. The first thousand years of the last period are divided into ages of gold, silver, steel and iron, the last age being a time when evil will assault the world with renewed vigour. The purpose of this myth is to explain how God's good world can be so full of evil, darkness, pain suffering and death. The answer is that history is the battle-ground between God and all that is good and the devil and all that is evil.

But the purpose of the myth is not only to interpret the past, it also explains the present in such a way that men may hope for, and trust in, the future. With the fall of the Sasanian empire the Zoroastrian religion faced enormous problems. It was not simply that there were mass conversions to Islam–caused either by sincerity, the hope of gain, or fear–the problem lay much deeper than that. According to the traditional myth the first saviour was expected one thousand years after Zoroaster. With the generally accepted date of Zoroaster that meant the saviour should have come about the year AD 400. But in the seventh century the Persian empire collapsed and with it, it seemed, the religion. There was a crisis of faith. Was it that God had deserted them? Was it that their whole religion was false? The writers of the Pahlavi books try to answer these questions; they seek to reconcile myth and history.

There are two ways in which the Pahlavi writers tackle the burning question of their day. One text, the *Bahman Yasht,* accounts for the delay in the coming of the saviour by inserting three additional periods into the traditional four which precede his coming. To the ages symbolised by gold, silver, steel and iron are added, after the age of steel, those of brass, copper and lead. Although this answered the question of why the saviour had not come–with the answer that he was still not due–it did not answer the deeper question

King Gayomart as he appears in an illustration from a manuscript of the Shah name.

برفت و بدو داد تخت و کلاه
بزرگی و دیهیم و گنج و سپاه
نهان گشت و گیتی برو شد سیاه
سپردش بضحاک تخت و کلاه
جهان زیر فرمان ضحاک شد
ز مهر نامه نام جم پاک شد
چو صد سالش اندر جهان کس ندید
ز چشم همه مردمان ناپدید
صدم سال روزی بدریای چین
پدید آمد آن شاه ناپاک دین
نهان بود چند از بد اژدها
نیامد بفرجام زو هم رها
چو ضحاکش آورد ناگه بچنگ
یکایک ندادش زمانی درنگ
باره مر او را بدو نیم کرد
جهان را ازو پاک و بی بیم کرد
شد آن تخت شاهی و آن دستگاه
زمانه ربودش چو بیجاده کاه
ازو پیش بر تخت شاهی بود
وزان رنج بردن چه آمدش سود
گذشته برو سالیان هفتصد
پدید آورید همه نیک و بد
چه باید همی زندگانی دراز
که گیتی نخواهد گشادنت راز
همی پروراندت با شهد و نوش
جز آواز نرمت نیاید بگوش
یکایک چو جویی که گسترد مهر
بخواهد نمودن ببد نیز چهر
همه راز دل برگشادی بدو
بدلت اندر از درد خون آورد

of whether God had failed in the hour of need, the time of the Islamic invasion. It is to this question that the compilers of the *Bundahishn* and the *Denkard* address themselves in certain chapters. The ancient Avestan scheme of history taught that the age of iron would be a period of distress, when the religion would decline, social and family life would distintegrate and disorder would be rampant everywhere, not just on earth, but in the cosmos also, in the form of drought and pestilence. The Pahlavi writers see in the invasion of Persia the fulfilment or working out of this scheme. The invaders are called 'demons' and they are the brood of the demons of greed. They break up families, causing harm and distress. To the compilers the invaders represented the outbreak of demonic forces expected in the last century of the millennium. The writer of one text, therefore, looked for signs of the cosmic disorder that he believed must accompany this onslaught. Seeing no such obvious signs he warned that they must be happening in secret.

pestilence is secretly advancing and deceiving so that deaths become more numerous
Dk. VII, 8, 19

Thus the *Bundahishn* and the *Denkard,* despite their initial appearance of being dry academic collections of ancient myths, are in fact powerful appeals and messages of comfort to the faithful. They are preaching the message that the terror which many face, the threat to life and home, is not unforeseen or beyond the power of god to overcome. The faith, the message runs, is not in vain. Men must hold fast and take heart, for this is the fulfilment of the millennium. Soon a prince will come who will restore Iran; the saviour will be born and God will overthrow the devil and all the demons.

Although these texts are compilations of ancient material, this material was adapted to meet the spiritual needs of Zoroastrians in a specific situation. Their interpretations of traditional myths in the light of contemporary history provide a stake to which the faithful can cling and a message of hope for the future.

Reconstructing History from Myth

The ancient myths of the dragon-slaying heroes were adapted to history in a totally different way from the prophetic adaptation of the myths concerning the end of the world. The later Persian texts and early Muslim historians used the myths of Gayomart, Yima and the rest as a base for a legendary history of Persia from the day of creation to the time of the Islamic invasion. This use of myth is perhaps more interesting for the poetic form given to the history by Firdausi in the *Shah name,* but even in this work much of the spirit of the ancient dualism is retained. The following outline of this 'history' is based almost entirely on the *Shah name*.

Gayomart, the first man of the Zoroastrian myth of creation, appears as the first king who ruled over the whole world. His home was in the mountains and he is pictured wearing leopard skins. Clothing and food were discovered by him and he was reverenced by all, a reverence which gave rise to religion. His rule, which lasted for thirty years, was as benevolent as the sun while Gayomart himself was great in majesty and power. Hoshang was the grandson of Gayomart and heir to his throne. He was entrusted with the task of exacting vengeance on the black demon for the murder of his father Siyamak. Hoshang's army consisted of wild and tame animals, birds and supernatural beings, and with it he routed the army of the black demon and cut the villain's head off. With this victory achieved, the aged Gayomart was able to die in peace and the victorious Hoshang assumed his throne of splendour. Three gifts for mankind arose from his reign: the use of metal, farming and fire. Regarding the last, the *Shah name* reports that as Hoshang was riding out to the mountains one day he was confronted by an elongated creature black in colour:

In its head were two eyes like pools of blood and from its mouth there poured black smoke covering the earth with gloom
Levy p. 7

His glory and power gone, Jamshid, the ancient Yima, is sawn in two on the orders of the tyrant Zahhak.

right *The evil Zahhak seated on his throne. The snakes implanted on the tyrant's shoulders by the Evil One needed human brains for their daily food.*

far right *The great king Faridun with his two sons to whom he gave the rule of the world.*

چون عارض تو ماه نباشد روشن
فرخی گفت
مانند رخت گل نبود در گلشن
مژگانت همی گذر کند از جوشن
عسجدی گفت
فردوسی گفت
مانند سنان گیو در جنگ پشن

پرستیدن مهرگان دین او | تن آسانی و خوردن آیین او | اگر یادگار است از او ماه و مهر | بکوش و برنج ایچ منمای چهر
ورا بد جهان سالیان پنج صد | نیفگند یک روز بنیاد بد | جهان چون برو بر نماند ای پسر | نماند بتو نیز اندُه مخور
فرانک نه آگاه بد زین نهان | که فرزند او شاه بد در جهان | ز ضحاک شد تخت شاهی تهی | سر آمد برو روزگار مهی
پس آگاهی آمد ز فرخ پسر | بمادر که فرزند شد تاجور | نیایش کنان شد سر و تن بشست | به پیش جهاندار آمد نخست
نهاد آن دو رخسار بر خاک بر
همیخواند نفرین بضحاک بر
همی آفرین کرد بر کردگار
بدان شادمان گردش روزگار
هر آنکس که بودی از آن بی نیاز | همی داشت روز بد خویش راز | نهانش نوا کرد و با کس نگفت | همی راز او داشت اندر نهفت
یکی هفته زین گونه بخشید چیز | چنان شد که درویش نشناخت نیز | دگر هفته بزم را ساز کرد | مهان را که بودند آواز کرد

far left *His forces defeated, the wicked Zahhak is led in chains before the triumphant hero, Faridun.*

left *Faridun enthroned in a flower garden after his victory over Zahhak.*

Hoshang threw a stone at the creature. The stone hit another stone and produced a spark, the creature was destroyed and fire was born. Hoshang's son, Takhmoruw, reigned for thirty years, in which time he subjugated the demons so that he was able to pass on to his son Yima (Jamshid in the *Shah name*) a world of peace.

Jamshid organised mankind into the various social classes. He set apart priests, established the warrior class, deputed some to be husbandmen and others to be concerned with the various crafts. He himself was both king and priest and introduced a number of beneficial products into the world: the craft of spinning and weaving, medicines and precious jewels. In his reign all was peace and plenty, the demons were made to toil and labour, men had no need to work and no one died. Jamshid fashioned himself a royal throne and had the demons lift it in the air so that

he sat upon that throne like the sun in the firmament. To celebrate, that day was called a new day–the festival of Now-ruz–the first day of the year.
Levy p. 10

But Jamshid became conceited, he recited his achievements and declared that men should entitle him creator of the world. At this men deserted his court and his glory disappeared. The future appeared black.

The story is now transferred to the court of a much respected prince, Merdas. Merdas had a brave and active son, Zahhak. One day the devil appeared at the court in the guise of a visitor and beguiled Zahhak with his talk. The innocent youth swore an oath never to divulge the words of the devil and to obey his commands. The devil, tempting the youth with visions of regal power, persuaded him to kill his father and take the throne.

The devil then appeared to Zahhak in the form of a cook and led him astray by giving him meat to eat. Until this time men had been vegetarians. The devil asked that he might kiss the shoulders of so great a monarch, beguiling the youth with flattery. When he had done so the devil disappeared into the ground and two black snakes grew from the shoulders of the king. As often as he cut them off, they grew again until the devil, this time in the form of a doctor, said that the only remedy was to feed the snakes every day with human brains.

و بر سریر دولت و اریکهٔ سلطنت ممکن شد دختر ضحاک را در عقد نکاح آورد و در مدت دو سال دو پسر از او متولد شد
یکی را تور نام نهاد و دیگری را سلم و هر دو عظیم بدخوی و لجوج و کج طبع و حقود بودند و بعد از آن بچندگاه ایرج از دختر
شاه فارسی ایراندخت نام متولد شد و ایرج چون از قید مهد و مدام و بند رضاعت و فطام رهائی یافت مخایل اهل تمیز در شمایل
او ظاهر شده رغبت آموختن علم رمایت و دانستن آداب فروسیت محرض طبع و مهیج نفس او بود تا اندک زمانی در آن صنعت ماهر و استاد
و حاذق و چالاک گشت و چون اکثر اوقات با خداوندان فضل و هنر مجالست و مکالمت می نمود از محاورت ایشان نیز نصیبی
وافر و بهرهٔ کامل حاصل کرد و بر ملازمت خدمت پدر مواظبت می نمود و شرایط آداب در انقیاد و مطاوعت او بتقدیم
می رسانید و پدر چون بگوشهٔ چشم و نظر صادرات افعال و واردات اقوال او مشاهده می کرد آثار نجابت و شهامت
و دلایل یمن و سعادت در حرکت و سکون او چون آب و آینه معاینه میدید و هنوز در مقتبل کار و فاتحهٔ بلوغ و ریعان عمر
و عنفوان جوانی بود که اعیان ملک و اشراف حضرت بتقدیم او در رمایت حزم و فطانت رای و حصافت عقل و کمال
مردی و مردمی معترف شدند و در تصاریف امور مملکت و مغالیق ابواب سلطنت از انوار هدایت و آثار فضایل او مقتبس
و مغترف گشت و فریدون در اعظام حال او زیادت از فرزندان دیگر می کوشید و این معنی ضمیمهٔ عداوت برادران
می شد تا روزی باتفاق موبدان مجلس و ملازمان درگاه و مهتران سپاه مجمعی ساخت و وضیع و شریف را در آن مجلس جمع کرده

خطبه بزبان خویش که ترجمهٔ آن بلسان عرب این است ادا کرد الحمد لله المتفرد بالکمال والبقا المتوحد بالعظمة
والبهاء المتعالی عن الاکفاء والنظراء احمده علی جمیع الافضال واشکره علی جزیل النوال واتوکل علیه
فی جمیع الاحوال وارغب الیه بالتضرع والابتهال ایها الناس نحن ارباب الملک وسواس الرعایا یحمیکم من اعدائکم
ویبادر الی ما یدعو بالرفق بکم ونجتهد فی حصول منافعکم ودفع مضارکم فالویل ثم الویل لمن لم یکن من حزبنا
ولا یخاف من باسنا اتقوا الحسد فانه یورث النکال واجتنبوا البغی فانه یرجع الی نفسه وکونوا اخوانا مترادفین واعوانا
مساعدین واقول قولی هذا واستغفر الله العظیم وچون شاه فریدون از تقریر این خطبه بپرداخت روی بحاضران
جمع و مقیمان مجلس آورد و گفت بدانید که سپری و کهن سالی بر من زور آورده است و ضعف شیبت و شیخوخیت در من اثر کرده

As Zahhak increased in power Jamshid's authority declined and men proclaimed Zahhak the monarch of Persia. Jamshid went into hiding but was at last found in the sea of China where Zahhak had him sawn in two, thus ridding the world of him. Zahhak's rule lasted for a thousand years, a thousand years of oppression, in which virtue declined, sorcery increased and each day two men died that their brains might be fed to the serpents who grew from Zahhak's shoulders.

But all was not well for Zahhak. In a dream he foresaw the birth of Faridun (Thraetaona) and sought to have the child destroyed, but in vain. Fearful of so mighty an opponent, Zahhak commanded that an army of demons be gathered to attack his enemy and a proclamation made to affirm his virtue as king. No one dared oppose so mighty a monarch, until one day a humble blacksmith, wronged by the king, appeared at court seeking a just release for his imprisoned son. He proclaimed

Although you have a dragon's form, you are a king and it is your duty to let me have justice.
Levy p. 18

The king was astonished at the outburst and acceded to his request but sought in return his signature of the proclamation. The blacksmith, a brave and forthright man, refused, denounced the king, and with his son raised an army for Faridun from the market place. His banner was a strip of leather decorated with jewels and for Faridun he prepared a mace with an ox's head. Leaving his palace whose pinnacles reached the skies, Faridun led his forces through torrents and over deserts to the palace of the wicked king in Jerusalem. Unafraid at the sight of the palace which reached up to the planet Saturn, he grasped his mace and advanced. Zahhak was absent, but on hearing of Faridun's invasion and the setting free of Jamshid's sisters he rode at breathtaking speed before a mighty army. With his army before the city Zahhak entered the palace himself, unrecognised in his heavy armour. As he approached the women with murder in his heart Faridun 'advanced upon him with the speed of a storm wind' and smashed his helmet with his mace. Warned by an angel, he refrained from killing the evil tyrant, but bound him and with trusted companions carried him off to Mount Demavend. Now ruler of the world, Faridun turned his attention to improving the lot of men. His old mythological assault on disease is transformed, or demythologised, and becomes instead an agricultural act of overcoming pestilence with husbandry.

Here we must leave the narrative of the *Shah name* and the 'history' that it reconstructs from the ancient myths. But the process of interpreting myth as history is one which continues in Zoroastrianism and in the minds of the faithful of many religions to the present day. A famous Parsi scholar, for example, suggests that Haoma, plant and god, was

a great man of Iran, who had done some great deeds that commemorated his name.
Modi, RC., p. 301

Myth and history are, then, completely intertwined in Zoroastrian belief. The Persians understand the whole of their history, past, present and future in the light of their mythology. History is the stage for the battle between good and evil and the events which take place on that stage can only be truly appreciated when seen against the backcloth of God's purpose and nature.

Firdausi, the poet of the Shah name*, discoursing with other court poets.*

A tower of silence or dakhma, *high up on a hillside. Dead bodies are exposed in* dakhmas *to the vultures so that the corruption of death, the handiwork of the devil, may not defile the sacred elements of earth, fire or water.*

MYTH, RITUAL AND SYMBOLISM

In Zoroastrianism an act of sacrifice, or the correct performance of a ritual, has a value and power in and of itself. Ritual acts are effective sources of power that aid the gods as well as men. So, as we have seen (pp. 31–2), Tishtrya is unable to defeat the demon of drought and produce the life-giving waters until sacrifice has been offered to him. Similarly Zurvan, when wanting a son, offered sacrifice although he himself is the absolute and there is no one to whom he could present his offerings. A sacrifice offered with devotion is one of the most meritorious acts a Zoroastrian can perform. Without sacrifice the world would cease to exist, but by it the power of Ahriman is reduced. At the renovation men will be made immortal through a sacrifice offered by Ohrmazd himself. This understanding of sacrifice, still dominant in Zoroastrianism, dates back to Indo-Iranian times, for sacrifice is central to the religion of the earliest of Indian texts, the *Vedas,* where duly performed rituals are thought to be effective independent of the will of the gods. In Zoroastrian ritual every word and action is imbued with the highest significance. The reasons for many of the rituals have been forgotten and the actions are given a significance that they may not have had originally, but perhaps the reader is more interested in what Zoroastrians believe now than in a historical reconstruction of the most ancient beliefs.

A good example of the symbolism that is attached to religious objects is that surrounding the *Kushti*, a thread with which every Zoroastrian is invested at initiation. The Kushti is made up of seventy-two threads which are said to symbolise the seventy-two chapters of the book of the *Yasna.* At the end are three tassels, each composed of twenty-four threads which are said to symbolise the twenty-four sections of the *Visparat,* a part of the liturgical prayer. The seventy-two threads are woven into six strands, each strand symbolising the six religious duties of the Zoroastrian. The twelve threads in each strand symbolise the months of the year, the six tassels the great festivals, the hollow inside the thread is:

the space between this world and the next; the doubling of the thread in the beginning symbolises the connection between the present corporeal world and the future spiritual world; the turning of the Kushti inside out (during prayers) symbolises the passage of the soul from the corporeal to the spiritual world;

Sarvar Khanom weaving a Kushti, *the sacred thread worn by Zoroastrians, in Sharifabad, one of the most orthodox villages of Yazd.*

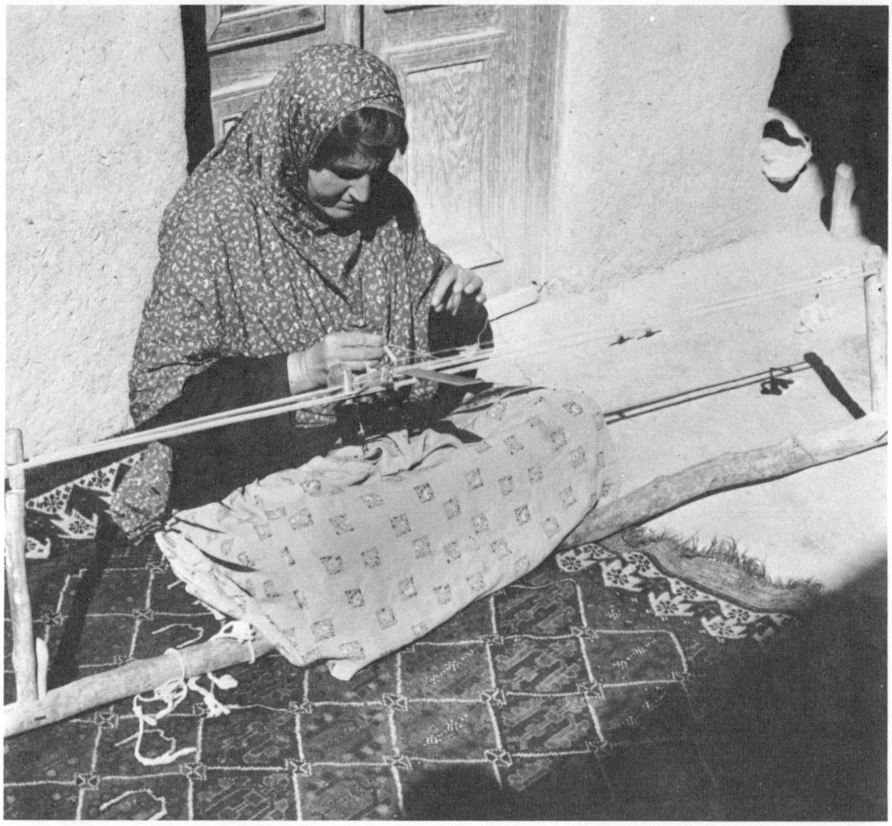

A seven-year-old girl being invested with the Kushti. *At the investiture ritual (the* Naojte*) the child affirms his or her resolve, is blessed and is thus received into the Zoroastrian faith. From that day forward the child is held to be morally responsible for all its actions and is henceforth bound to the faith.*

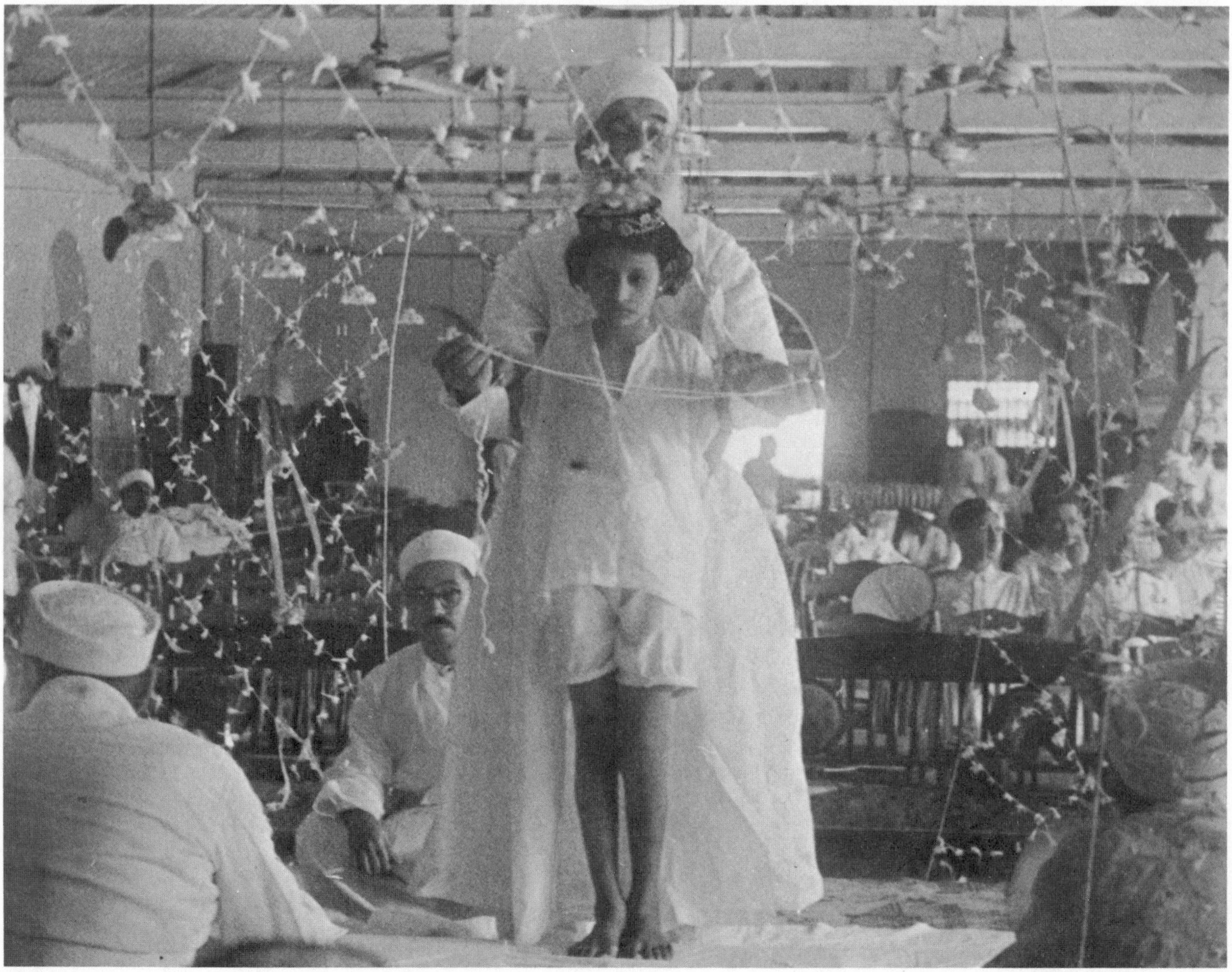

the final knotting of all the threads into one symbolises the universal brotherhood or union.
Modi, RC, pp. 185f

It is impossible in a short book to consider the inter-connection between myth and all the rituals of Zoroastrianism. Instead we shall look at three of the most important of the rituals: those connected with death, Fire and Haoma.

The Funerary Rites

The funerary rites of Zoroastrianism are very clearly governed by the mythology. Death, it will be remembered, is the work of the devil in Zoroastrian belief. It is his triumph over the Good Creation. A dead body is, therefore, the abode of demons. The more righteous the deceased the greater the triumph of Ahriman and the greater the demonic power necessary to achieve it. Hence the corpse of a holy man is a far greater source of defilement than that of a wicked man whose death was easily achieved. Many of the funerary rites are concerned with purification from the contamination which is the work of demons. Since a corpse is such a source of defilement it cannot be allowed to be buried for fear of contaminating the sacred element of the earth, nor can it be burned for fear of defiling the fire. (One exception to the last point is the modern method of cremation where it is not an actual flame but intense heat generated by electricity that consumes the body.) Wherever possible, therefore, bodies are exposed in towers of silence, *dahkmas,* for the vultures to consume.

The belief in the passage of the soul in the first three days after death determines the rites which are performed. As it is Sraosha who protects the

At the same time that the child is invested with the Kushti *he or she is also invested with the* Sadre *or shirt. The putting on of the shirt symbolises the donning of the Good Religion. The* Sadre *must be worn next to the skin and at all times. In front of the young initiate burns the sacred flame.*

An Irani Zoroastrian priest standing before the sacred flame in a fire temple in Persia. His mouth is covered to prevent his defiling the fire with his breath.

soul during this time, prayers are offered to him during the five divisions of the day by two or more priests and the relatives both at home and in the Fire-Temple. The most important of these prayers is the one offered on the third day when the soul passes to its judgment. Then the blessing of the Almighty is sought and ceremonies are offered to the angels concerned with the judgment.

The rites for the deceased do not end three days after death, but the stress is not on continued mourning. Excessive mourning is a sin in Zoroastrianism for it is of no help to the soul, it can harm the body of the living, and is pointless in view of the belief in a life after death and the assurance of the resurrection. Zoroastrians have a strong sense of communion with the dead, who are invited to share in the feastings of the living, not in grief but in companiable happiness, 'for the rejoicing of the soul'. A scholar who has lived among the Zoroastrians gives an interesting insight into this attitude:

After I had enjoyed for some time the hospitality of Irani Zoroastrians, but before I had begun to comprehend this feeling for the dead, I ventured, still haunted by associations of death with sorrow, to ask if they never celebrated a feast day without an accompanying ritual for the dead. The reply, made with mild astonishment, was: 'But of course not. We always want them to share in our happiness.'
M. B. Pious Foundations, p. 247, n4

The Zoroastrian mythology of the individual and universal judgments thus dictates both the funerary rites and their attitude to festivities.

The Fire Ritual

The Zoroastrian myth concerning the personification of Fire, Atar, has already been discussed (pp. 37–8). We can now look at the mythology of some of the sacred fires of the ritual. Most religions try to trace the origins of their great centres of ritual back to the early times of their sacred history. The Zoroastrians try to trace their three most famous fires back to primeval history. These three fires are the Farnbag fire, which is said to have been situated either in Kabul in modern Afghanistan or Kanya in Persia; the

To this day the fire forms the centre of many Hindu rituals. Here a group of Hindus in a temple in Newcastle upon Tyne chant the sacred words over the fire before pouring melted butter on to it.

Gushnasp fire, which was probably situated in Shiz, and the Burzen Mihr fire, which was situated on Mount Revand in the north west of Nishapur. All three are said to have been carried on the back of the mythical ox, Srishok, in the reign of the primeval Takhmoruw. One night there was a great storm and the fires were blown off the ox's back into the sea where they continued to burn and give light to men at sea. Each fire is associated with one of the three classes of society, the Farnbag with the priests, the Gushnasp with the warriors and the Burzen Mihr with the productive workers. All three helped Yima in his paradisal kingdom and it was Yima who installed the Farnbag fire in its due place. When his glory fell it was that fire which saved his glory from the evil Dahak. The Burzen Mihr fire protected the world until the time of Zoroaster's patron, Vishtaspa, preparing the way for the great revelation and itself performing miracles during the great monarch's rule. The Gushnasp fire is said to have preserved the world until the time of the great Sasanian king, Khusrau. When he destroyed idol temples the fire settled on his horse's mane dispelling the darkness and gloom. These three great fires, then, are not thought to have been simply late historical innovations but are rather the protectors and guides for men throughout history.

There are three classes of ritual fires, Bahram fires, the Adaran fires and the Dadgah fires. The Bahram is the victorious king of fires. It is invoked, in the name of Ohrmazd, to give strength against the forces of darkness for its glory does battle with the Lie, standing as it does as a symbol of righteousness. The fire is enthroned rather than installed and the wood is set out in the pattern of a throne. Over it hangs a crown expressing thr sovereignty of the mighty fire. When it has been enthroned it is carried in triumph like a king by four priests in procession, while others hold a canopy over it. Before and behind proceed priests with swords and maces of Mithra, all forming a royal bodyguard. Once enthroned it can only be tended by priests who have undergone the most rigorous purification rites. No one but they can enter the sanctuary and even they must tend it with white-gloved hands. The reason for its sanctity is the great process of purification. Sixteen fires are gathered from different sources and then purified a total of 1,128 times, a process which takes about a year. The cost involved is enormous and not surprisingly such a fire is very rarely enthroned.

The Adaran and Dadgah fires are much less grand affairs. The latter can even be tended by laymen, yet both are installed with martial honours, for the sacred fires represent the spiritual rule of light and truth in the war against the powers of darkness, a battle which the faithful must fight in collaboration with Ohrmazd and his son, Fire. The fires of all classes serve as reminders that as they must be purified so too must man. Equally, a famed Parsi argues, they remind men that as the wood is collected from all different grades of society, so all men are equal before God, no matter what their social class, providing they pass through the process of purification. When a Parsi approaches the fire he marks his forehead with some ash as a reminder that he, like the fire, will eventually turn to dust, and he prays:

Let me do my best to spread, like this fire, before my death, the fragrance of charity and good deeds and lead the light of righteousness and knowledge before others.
Modi, R.C. p. 229

Haoma, the Ritual Offering

As the fire may not be seen by unbelieving eyes, so also only believers may join in the ritual offering of haoma. We have already seen something of the interconnection of myth and ritual associated with this figure, at once plant, god, priest and sacrificial victim (see pp.). In ancient India the ritual process is compared to the great fertilising, or life-giving process of nature, thus the sieve through which the juice of the plant is strained represents the sky, the juice pouring into the water and milk represents the sun, but because it is golden in colour it is also likened to lightning and the noise of the process to thunder. Yet again it is compared to a bull and the juice entering the waters is a symbol of the fertilisation of a herd of cows. Rain, storn, sun and fertility are all represented by soma, a perfect illustration of the interconnection of myth and ritual and of the variety of symbols which can be seen within one myth or ritual.

In Persia the haoma ritual is part of the great Yasna sacrifice. For the offering the priest sits cross-legged. The haoma plant is pounded and the juice is

Children gathering bundles of haoma, the sacred plant, which grows on the mountains of Persia.

A bucket used for the sacred haoma in the holy ritual meal of Zoroastrianism in which the god is at once the priest and the victim who gives life to men.

far left *The Sasanian fire altars at Naqsh-i Rustam illustrate the Zoroastrian practice of worshipping in the mountains, as well as pointing to the antiquity of the reverence for fire among both Zoroastrians and Hindus.*

pressed through a filter made from the hair of a sacred bull, to be mixed with consecrated water. The ritual is long, complicated and full of symbolic acts. The haoma is pounded four times to symbolise the coming of Zoroaster and his three sons, the saviours. The consecrated water is poured out three times, symbolising the three processes of rain: evaporation, the formation of clouds and condensation as rain. During the ritual the metal mortar is struck three times to symbolise the presence of good thoughts, good words and good deeds. Thus the mythical setting (the reference to the saviours) and the cosmic setting (the giving of rain) are integrated with the ethical setting in a way that is wholly typical of the Zoroastrian faith. Although the liturgy is recited in a dead language, Avestan, which very few understand, the emphasis for all is that the mind, the source of every action, should be kept pure.

The Understanding of Myth and Ritual

The ancient myths of Zoroastrianism, as in almost all religions, remain the mainspring of the daily religious life of the faithful. They provide the justification for actions, however the modern intellectual may re-interpret or adapt the tradition. Naturally the leaders claim that their symbolic interpretation of the myth is both relevant to man's daily life and true to the original intention of the myth. In what religion would one dare to suggest that the interpretation given to a particular myth was not that of the founder but a completely new idea!

In the preservation of the ancient practices Zoroastrianism provides a particularly good example of the conservative character of ritual. What we

This portrayal of Magi offering sacrifice is of the fifth century BC and comes from Dascylium, or Eregli, in Asia Minor. The accurate representation of the scene—the barsom twigs, the covered mouth and the animal heads—is evidence of how far and wide their practices were known.

have seen in Zoroastrianism is only a form writ large of what may be observed in most religions, including those of the West. Zoroastrianism is, as we shall see, very much a common-sense religion in its understanding of man and the world; it is profound and rather philosophical. That it can also retain such a traditional and conservative attitude to its myth and ritual makes it an interesting 'case book' to study. It contains a number of particularly clear examples of how religions tend to develop. The modern critical mind finds it difficult, if not impossible, to accept some of the myths and rituals of the traditional faiths, yet equally the faithful will not reject them. Instead they resort to allegory or symbolism, be it symbolic interpretation of the *Book of Genesis* or of the *Avesta*. The attempts of a modern Parsi to interpret the *Avesta* in modern terms rather than reject it is an interesting phenomenon which could be paralleled in many religions. Such a Parsi writes:

Some portions of the *Avesta,* if taken literally, would seem absurd. Mountains, rivers and similar topographical features do not refer to any physical locations, but probably to some psycho-physiological features, some psychic currents within the human body (brain, nerves or some plexus or gland etc.).
Quoted D-G, Symbols, p. 19

There is a lot of truth in the saying that as critical reflection develops symbolism tends to expand (Duchesne-Guillemin). This is true of the quotation just given and true of the Zoroastrian ritual, although we should not forget that the ancient mind also made extensive use of symbolism. Not all symbolic interpretations are necessarily modern.

In Zoroastrianism, then, myth and ritual are completely intertwined. The one supports, explains and justifies the other. Both preserve exremely ancient views of the world and of man's part in it. Yet neither are merely expressions of opinion. They are, together, effective sources of power which if properly recited and performed by men, themselves endowed with due power, bring benefit and merit to the individual in life, protection at death, and the promise of future bliss, and uphold the very existence of the universe. The vital nature of ritual action demands that everything be performed in precisely the right way. A wrong action, a mistake at any stage, could vitiate the whole act. The rituals are of such a sacred and potent character that unbelieving eyes cannot be allowed to see them.

Within the Zoroastrian ritual one can see the basic Zoroastrian beliefs, which are expressed in narrative form in the myths, acted out by the believers in the ritual. Zoroastrianism is a religion concerned with war, war against the powers of evil. The history of the world is, mythically speaking, a battle between good and evil: between God and the devil. So in the installation of the sacred fires, the symbol of the presence of God, martial imagery is very much to the fore. It is also a religion of hope. This hope is expressed in narrative form in the myths of the triumph of good over evil at the renovation, and is implicit in the ritual with its greater emphasis on prayers and rituals intended to aid the soul than on mourning, and its joyous invitation to the deceased to share in feasts.

To the modern Western mind the Zoroastrian attitude towards the ritual may appear rather magical. To the Zoroastrian the acts they perform have such power because they follow the pattern of a heavenly model, because they effectively unite the divine and human worlds, a common theme in their mythology. In view of their belief in the power of the ritual it is understandable that they should be reluctant to change its form, although in the interpretation given to their actions and myths we can see the modern critical mind at work.

A bull-headed mace of Mithra carried by Zoroastrian priests as a symbol of the war they must wage against the forces of evil. Mithra shakes his mace over hell three times each day to restrain the demons from inflicting greater punishment on the damned than they merit.

CONCLUSION: MYTH AND BELIEF

The Understanding of God, the World and Man

Myth, we have said, is important for what it means to the believer, for the reflections it contains on man's views on himself, the world and God. Myths are not bogus historical narratives. One must leave behind the outer shell of myth and look at the kernel. What is the kernel of Persian mythology and what views on life do the myths contain?

To a Zoroastrian, God is wholly good. Being fundamentally opposed to evil he can have no contact with it and is, throughout history, engaged in a life and death struggle with it. God is the source of all that is good, the creator of the heavens, the world and man, the source of life, health, beauty and joy. Evil is a reality, but a wholly negative force seeking to destroy, corrupt and defile. Death, disease, misery and sin are all the work of the devil who seeks to annihilate God's world.

The world is created by God as an aid in the battle against evil. He is a rational being and has a reason for all that he does. He does not create the world merely for sport, as in some branches of Hinduism, nor does he repent of it as the God of the Old Testament so often does. The world may be the battleground between good and evil, but it is essentially good, and when not corrupted by evil it displays the characteristics of its creator–orderliness and harmony. To deny the essential goodness of the material world is one of the gravest sins a Zoroastrian can commit. Doctrines which teach that the flesh is evil, that the body is a prison of the soul or of original sin are verbiage to a Zoroastrian. Therefore, he does not look to the final subjugation of the body or of matter, but to the ideal union of matter and spirit; he looks not for the end of the world, but for the renovation of God's world.

The creation and eschatological myths of Zoroastrianism provide the ultimate charter for the daily lives of the faithful. If the world belongs to God then it would be a sin for them to withdraw from it by becoming monks or ascetics. If God is characterised by creativity and increase then men have a religious duty to work for the increase of the Good Creation through agriculture, industry and marriage. Celibacy is a sin for it fails to expand the Good Creation. Abortion and homosexuality are sins for they prevent the true purpose of the sexual act, the increase of the Good Creation, just as effectively

The Irani Zoroastrian shrine of Herisht near Sharifabad, an orthodox village near Yazd. The villagers are gathered together for a feast day. It is interesting that mountain shrines retain their importance even today.

as the sinful abstinence of man's first parents did. Disease and ill-health are blights with which the devil afflicted the world at the beginning. Men, therefore, have a religious duty to preserve their bodies in a state of health. Man is composed of five elements–soul, vital spirit (the principle of life), fravashi (his heavenly self), consciousness and body, but he is a unity. Spiritual and physical health, therefore, go hand in hand. The idea that spiritual progress can be made by suppressing the body through fasting is sheer folly to the Zoroastrian. Since the material world belongs to God, material success that is gained honestly, without hurt to others, and is coupled with generosity, is an aid, not a hindrance, to spiritual progress. Unlike many of the contemplative schools of Hinduism, Zoroastrianism has an activist ethic. Idleness is of the devil and

work is the salt of life. Without work our life is idle and useless. Our religion teaches us that work is the aim and object of life. We must always keep our body ready and healthy for doing the duties of our life, to do good and right deeds, to help others and to fight against ignorance, evil and misery in the world.
Modi Catechism, p. 30

It was the devil who afflicted the world with misery. The religious attitude to life is, therefore, one of joy. On the day of the month that is dedicated to God the faithful are exhorted to 'drink wine and be merry', and on the day dedicated to Rashnu, the god of judgment, 'life is gay: do in holiness anything you will.' (*Counsels of Adherbadh ZT. pp. 107f.*) Debauchery, drunkeness and licence are, of course, equally condemned for all must be governed by the Golden Mean, by the motto 'all things in moderation'.

Man, as the great creation and ally of God, is the particular object for the onslaughts of evil. It is the duty of the faithful to overcome these assaults, to

overcome doubts and unrighteous desires with reason, overcome greed with contentment, anger with serenity, envy with benevolence, want with vigilance, strife with peace, falsehood with truth.
Counsels of the Sages, ZT p. 25

Dastur Khodadad Neryosangi, a Zoroastrian priest, saying the sunset prayers in the mountains.

The demons may assail man with disease, with all manner of afflictions, even with death, but, like the sinless Gayomart before him, man must always hold fast to the religion. This means more than just a faithful observance of the ritual and the reading of the sacred scriptures–because the material world, the body and happiness are the creation of God it is man's religious duty to preserve, expand and enjoy them all.

This is the path of Truth. He who follows it is a follower of Truth, an *asha-van,* a member of the Good Religion. But Zoroastrians do not believe that men are compelled to do this. The fravashis of men are said in the myths to have agreed collectively to fight for Ohrmazd. Freedom of will for the individual is an essential part of Zoroastrianism. The ally of God man may be, but all men have to choose between the Truth and the Lie. Once made, the choice has to be made continually re-affirmed, for evil ever lurks at hand to mislead and destroy. A doctrine of pre-destination such as flourished in Zurvanism and Islam is held morally repugnant, for it detracts from the justice and goodness of God. Equally repugnant is the idea that one man can die to save all. If everyone is free to adopt good or evil then everyone must be judged according to their own thoughts, words and deeds and not those of another.

Thus the Zoroastrian myths of creation and renovation are not merely narratives concerned with the remote past or distant future. They express the basic view of the God-Man relationship and provide the *rationale* for the conduct of the faithful. They are not just narratives about a cosmic battle, but accounts of that battle which each man encounters in his own daily life, in his marriage, in his work and in his religious life.

How, one may ask, does the believer interpret the myths concerning the gods and demons? What understanding of the God-Man relationship do these express? It must be remembered that the names of the divine and demonic powers often reflect abstract ideas, Vohu Manh (Good Mind), and Aka Manah (Evil Mind), Sraosha (Obedience) and Az (Wrong Mindedness). The cosmic battle becomes, then, a battle which each man must wage within himself in order to eject the Destructive Spirit from God's world. If men would expel the demons such as Wrath and Greed from their bodies then Ahriman would not be able to find a place in the world.

Ervad Firoze M. Kotwal wearing the white priestly robes and holding the sacred barsom twigs. The cloth in front of his mouth and nose is to prevent contamination of the twigs by his breath.

It is possible to put Ahriman out of this world in such a way that every person, for his own part, should chase him out of his body, for Ahriman's habitation in the world is in the bodies of men. Therefore when there is no habitation for him in the bodies of men, he is annihilated from the whole world. For as long as in this world (even) a small demon has his dwelling in a single person of men, Ahriman is in the world.
Dk. M. 6, 264, Shaked, Notes, p. 230

The duty of the Zoroastrian is not only stated in negative terms of expelling demons from one's self, it is also stated positively. The gods must be made to live in the bodies of men. The abstract qualities which represent the divine powers, Good Mind, Obedience, Truth, must be realised in the daily lives of men if men are to obtain the highest goal, if they are to be united with the gods. In one text it is said that the god whom the individual worships and reverences becomes the soul of that worshipper. When a man is activated by a particular spirit, be that spirit good or evil, then he becomes the material dwelling-place of that spirit and the worldly manifestation of its nature. Thus the battle between the gods and demons is seen as a battle between the passions and tensions at work in the individual. Man's innermost fears and problems are interpreted in the light of the cosmic process. This interpretation of myth, almost taking the myth out of mythology, 'de-mythologising' as modern theologians call it, may not have been the popular or general interpretation of the myths, as the demythologising of the New Testament is not the interpretation of the mass of people in most Christian churches. It may, however, be a very old tradition and appears to be the faith of Zoroaster himself. When Zoroaster speaks of the Bounteous Immortals, the archangels of later Zoroastrianism, the mythological element is negligible. He declares, for example, that whoever obeys Ahura Mazda

shall attain Integrity (Haurvatat) and Immortality (Ameretat)
through the deeds of the Good Mind (Vohu Manah).
Ys. 45:5, D-G, Hymns, p. 95

The high priest of Navsari, Dastur Meherji Rana, acknowledging the greetings of co-religionists.

Dastur Khodadad Neryosangi consecrating the fruits.

In another place he speaks of the rewards for good deeds and praises as

Truth (Asha), Immortality (Ameretat) and the Dominion (Kshathra)
of Integrity (Haurvatat).
Ys. 34:1, D-G, Hymns, p. 41

Here Zoroaster is speaking of the Entities, God's 'sons and daughters', in a way which is hardly mythological. It is an interpretation of myth which is meaningful to his hearers.

Zoroaster speaks of the Saviours, also, in a non-mythological way. He speaks of them as benefactors (the literal translation of Soshyants) who

Through Good Mind (Vohu Manah) strive in their deeds
To carry out the judgment which thou hast decreed, O Wise One,
as Truth (Asha),
For they were created the foes of Fury (Aeshma).
Ys. 48:12, D-G, Hymns, p. 39

In other words Zoroaster interprets the saviour not as a mythological figure but as anyone who works for Wisdom, Justice and the Good Religion in the world, thereby suppressing the disruptive forces at work within man.

Thus both Zoroaster and his followers see in the traditional mythology the pattern of the struggle which every man encounters within himself and in his daily life. Myth is viewed not simply as a narrative of what has happened or will happen, it is not an account of a remote external event, but an interpretation of the problems of human life. Perhaps many Zoroastrians throughout history have taken the myths at their face value, but if we were to look at them only on this simple level we would be doing a great disservice to the profundity which lies at the heart of much Persian mythology.

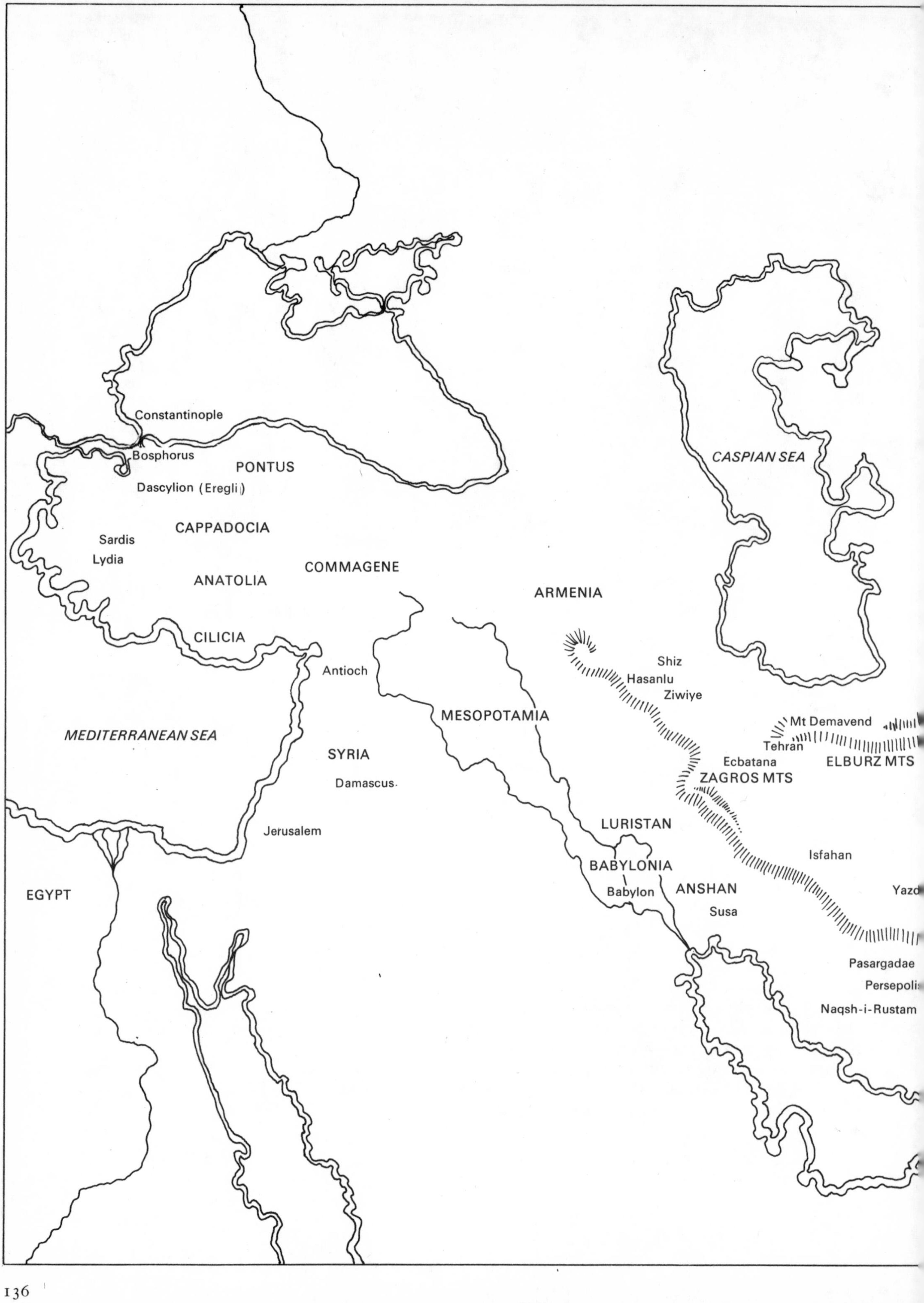

Constantinople
Bosphorus
PONTUS
Dascylion (Eregli)
CAPPADOCIA
Sardis
Lydia
ANATOLIA
COMMAGENE
ARMENIA
CASPIAN SEA
CILICIA
Antioch
Shiz
Hasanlu
Ziwiye
MESOPOTAMIA
Mt Demavend
Tehran
ELBURZ MTS
MEDITERRANEAN SEA
SYRIA
Ecbatana
ZAGROS MTS
Damascus
LURISTAN
Jerusalem
Isfahan
BABYLONIA
EGYPT
Babylon
ANSHAN
Susa
Pasargadae
Naqsh-i-Rustam

ANCIENT PERSIA
AND NEIGHBOURING COUNTRIES

LIST OF ABBREVIATIONS

AHM. I. Gershevitch, *The Avestan Hymn to Mithra,* for details see Bibliography.
AV. *Arda Viraf,* translated by Haug, for details see Bibliography.
BTA. B. T. Anklesaria, *Zand-Ākāsīh,* for details see Bibliography.
D-G Hymns. Duchesne-Guillemin, *The Hymns of Zarathustra,* for details see Bibliography.
D-G Symbols. Duchesne-Guillemin, *Symbols and Values in Zoroastrianism,* for details see Bibliography.
Dhalla, Nyashes. Dhalla, *The Nyaishes or Zoroastrian Litanies,* for details see Bibliography.
D.i.D. *Dadistan i Denik,* a Pahlavi text.
Dk. *Denkard,* a Pahlavi text.
Dk.M. Madan's edition of the *Denkard.*
G.Bd. The Greater or Iranian edition of the *Bundahishn,* a Pahlavi text.
Gershevitch. I. Gershevitch's article 'Iranian Literature', for details see Bibliography.
Gray, Foundations. Gray, *The Foundations of the Iranian Religions,* for details see Bibliography.
Kent. R. G. Kent, *Old Persian Grammar, Texts, Lexicon,* New Haven, 1953.
Levy. Levy, *The Epic of the Kings,* for details see the Bibliography.
Masani. Masani, *The Religion of the Good Life,* for details see the Bibliography.
MB. Pious Foundations. M. Boyce, 'The Pious Foundations of the Zoroastrians', *Bulletin of the School of Oriental and African Studies,* 31, 1968.
MEZ. Moulton, *Early Zoroastrianism,* for details see Bibliography.
M.Kh. *Mainog-i Khrad,* a Pahlavi text.
Modi, RC. Modi, *The Religious Ceremonies and Customs of the Parsees,* for details see Bibliography.
Modi, Cat. Modi, *Catechism of the Zoroastrian Religion,* for details see Bibliography.
MWS. Smith, Translation of the *Gathas,* for details see Bibliography.
Noss. J. B. Noss, *Man's Religions,* New York, 1968.
RV. *Rig-Veda,* an ancient Indian text.
S.B. *Shatapatha-Brahmana,* an ancient Indian text.
Shaked, Notes. S. Shaked, 'Some Notes on Ahreman, The Evil Spirit, and his Creation', in *Studies in Mysticism and Religion,* Studies in honour of G. Scholem, Jerusalem, 1967.
Wolff, *Das Avesta,* for details see Bibliography.
Ys. *Yasna* (Part of the Zoroastrian bible, the *Avesta*).
Yt. *Yasht* (Part of the Zoroastrian bible, the *Avesta*).
ZDT. Zaehner, *Dawn and Twilight of Zoroastrianism,* for details see Bibliography.
ZS.MB, R. *Zad Spram,* the particular text used in this book is translated by M. Boyce in 'Rapithwin, No Ruz, and the Feast of Sade', in *Pratidanam,* studies in honour of F. B. J. Kuiper, The Hague, 1968.
ZT. Zaehner, *Teachings of the Magi,* for details see Bibliography.

BIBLIOGRAPHY

Books in English
Anklesaria, B. T., *Zand-Ākāsīh,* Bombay, 1956
Zand-î Vohûman Yasn, Bombay, 1957
Arberry, A. J., *Legacy of Persia,* Oxford, 1963
Benveniste, E., *The Persian Religion According to the Chief Greek Texts,* Paris, 1929

Cameron, C. G., *History of Early Iran*, Chicago, 1936
Campbell, L. A., *Mithraic Iconography and Ideology*, Leiden, 1968
Carnoy, A. J., 'Iranian Mythology' in *Mythology of all Races*, vol. VI, ed. L. H. Gray, New York, 1964
Cumont, F., *The Mysteries of Mithra*, New York, 1956
Dhalla, N., *History of Zoroastrianism*, New York, 1928
The Nyaishes or Zoroastrian Litanies, New York, 1965
Duchesne-Guillemin, J., *The Hymns of Zarathustra*, London, 1952
The Western Response to Zoroaster, Oxford, 1958
Symbols and Values in Zoroastrianism, New York, 1966
Frye, R. N., *The Heritage of Persia*, London, 1962
Gershevitch, I., 'Iranian Literature' in *Literatures of the East*, Ed. E. B. Ceadel, London, 1953
The Avestan Hymn to Mithra, Cambridge, 1959
Ghirshman, R., *Iran*, London, 1961
Persia from the Origins to Alexander the Great, London, 1964
Iran, Parthians and Sasanians, London, 1962
Gray, L. H., *The Foundations of the Iranian Religions*, Bombay, 1925
Haug, M., and West, E. W., *The Book of Ardā Vīrāf*, Bombay-London, 1872-4
Henning, W. B., *Zoroaster, Politician or Witch-Doctor?* Oxford, 1951
Jackson, A. V. W., *Zoroaster, The Prophet of Ancient Iran*, New York, 1965
Zoroastrian Studies, New York, 1965
Levy, R., *The Epic of the Kings, Shāh-nāma*, London, 1967
Masani, R. P., *The Religion of the Good Life*, London, 1954
Modi, J. J., *The Religious Ceremonies and Customs of the Parsees*, Bombay, 1937
A Catechism of the Zoroastrian Religion, Bombay, 1962
Moulton, J. H., *Early Religious Poetry of Persia*, Cambridge, 1911
Early Zoroastrianism, London, 1913
The Treasure of the Magi, London, 1917
Pavry, J. D. C., *The Zoroastrian Doctrine of a Future Life*, New York, 1965,
Sacred Books of the East, vols 4, 5, 18, 23, 24, 31, 37, 47 contain translations of a number of Zoroastrian texts, some of which remain the only English translations available.
Smith, M. W., *Studies in the Syntax of the Gathaṣ of Zarathushtra Together with Text, Translation, and Notes*, New York, 1966,
Thieme, P., *Mitra and Aryaman*, New Haven, 1958
Vermaseren, M. J., *Mithras, The Secret God*, London, 1963
Corpus Inscriptionum et Monumentorum Religionis Mithriacae, The Hague, 1956, 1960
Zaehner, R. C., *Zurvan, A Zoroastrian Dilemma*, Oxford, 1955
The Teachings of the Magi, London, 1956
The Dawn and Twilight of Zoroastrianism, London, 1961

French Books
Christensen, A., *Les Types du premier Homme et du roi*, Stockholm-Leiden, 1917-1934
Cumont, F., *Textes et Monuments figurés relatifs aux mystères de Mithra*, I-II, Brussels, 1896-9
Duchesne-Guillemin, J., *La Religion de L'Iran Ancien*, Paris, 1962
Mole, M., *Culte, Mythe et Cosmologie dans L'Iran Ancien*, Paris, 1963
La legende de Zoroastre selon les textes Pehlevis, Paris, 1967
Varenne, J., *Zarathushtra et la tradition Mazdéenne*, Paris, 1966

German Books:
Hinz, W., *Zarathushtra*, Stuttgart, 1961
Humbach, H., *Die Gathas des Zarathustra*, Heidelberg, 1959
Lommel, H., *Die Yäst's des Awesta*, Göttingen, 1927
Die Religion Zarathushtras, Tübingen, 1930
Nyberg, H. S., *Die Religionen des alten Iran*, Osnabrück, 1966
Widengren, G., *Die Religionen Irans*, Stuttgart, 1965
Wolff, F., *Das Avesta Die Heiligen Bücher der Parsen*, Strassburg, Berlin, 1960,

ACKNOWLEDGMENTS

The illustrations in this book were reproduced by kind permission of the following:
American Numismatic Society, New York: 19; Archaeological Museum, Istanbul: 128; Archaeological Museum, Teheran: 26–27, 28 *bottom*, 29, 30, 44 *bottom*, 47 *left*; Atkins Museum (Nelson Fund) Kansas City: 25; Bäyerische Staatsbibliothek, Munich: 23; Chester Beatty Library, Dublin: 41, 94, 115; Bibliothèque Nationale, Paris: 63, 73, 116, 117; Bodleian Library, Oxford: 61, 112; British Museum: 5, 12, 22 *bottom*, 31, 37, 43, 45, 50, 52, 66, 100 *left*, 106, 118; Bürgermeisteramt Stadt Besigheim: 84; Gallery of Fine Arts, Yale University: 81 *top*; Hermitage Museum, Leningrad: 33, 44 *top*, 47 *right*; Dr B. Heükemes, Kupfälzisches Museum, Heidelberg: 83; The Metropolitan Museum of Art, New York: 40, 114 (gift of Alexander Smith Cochran), 46 (Rogers Fund); Musée Guimet, Paris: 36, 42, 110; Museum of Antiquities of the University of Newcastle-upon-Tyne: 76–77, 85 *bottom*, 85 *top* (Richmond Collection); Freer Gallery of Art, Washington, D.C.: 80; Staatliche Museen Preussischer Kulturbesitz: 32; The University Museum, Philadelphia: 28 *top*; Victoria and Albert Museum, London: 18, 39; Zemalski Museum, Sarajevo: 82

Photographs were supplied by the following:
Aerofilms, London: 10–11; Professor Sir Harold Bailey: 65; Barnabys, London: 2–3; Dr A. H. Bivar: 21, 43; Professor Mary Boyce: 20, 58, 59, 122 *top*, 127 *left*, 130, 133, 134, 135; C. M. Daniels: 51, 79 *right*, 85 *bottom*, 86, 87, 124, 132; John Dayton, London: 6–7, 99 *top*, 103, 104; Professor Dr F. K. Dörner, Münster: 34, 35, 83 *right*; Giraudon, Paris: 36, 42, 110; Holle Verlag, Baden-Baden: 19, 102, 109; Imperial Iranian Embassy, London: 90, 105 *bottom*; Mansell Collection, London: 74–75; Mansell-Alinari: 79 *left*; Inge Morath (Magnum): 107, 125; Antonello Perissinotto, Padua: 13, 15, 16 *bottom left*, 98, 101, 126; Popperfoto, London: 16 *top*, 93, 99, 100 *right*, 122 *bottom*, 123; Josephine Powell, Rome: 16 *bottom right*, 22 *top*, 24, 26–27, 28, 29, 30, 44, 55, 96, 108; Roger-Viollet, Paris: 17; Rex Roberts, Dublin: back jacket, 41, 94, 115; Scala, Florence: 88–89; Schäfer, Besigheim: 84; Roger Wood, London: front jacket, 14, 48, 68–69, 120–121; Weidenfeld and Nicholson: 44 *top*

INDEX

Numbers in italic refer to illustrations.